From Texas to Tinian and Tokyo Bay

# From Texas to Tinian and Tokyo Bay

## The Memoirs of Captain J.R. Ritter, Seabee Commander during the Pacific War, 1942–1945

Edited by
Jonathan Templin Ritter

Number 17 in the North Texas Military Biography
and Memoir Series

University of North Texas Press
Denton, Texas

Permissions:
University of North Texas Press
1155 Union Circle #311336
Denton, TX 76203-5017

The paper used in this book meets the minimum requirements of the American
National Standard for Permanence of Paper for Printed Library Materials,
z39.48.1984. Binding materials have been chosen for durability.

Library of Congress Cataloging-in-Publication Data
Ritter, J. R. (James Rex), 1902–1994, author. | Ritter, Jonathan Templin,
1983– editor.
    From Texas to Tinian and Tokyo Bay : the memoirs of Captain J. R.
Ritter, Seabee commander during the Pacific War, 1942-1945 / edited
by Jonathan Templin Ritter.
    pages cm.
Includes bibliographical references and index.
    ISBN-13 978-1-57441-771-5 (cloth)
    ISBN-13 978-1-57441-781-4 (ebook)
1. Ritter, J. R. (James Rex), 1902–1994. 2. United States. Navy. Seabees—
Officers—Biography. 3. World War, 1939–1945—Campaigns—Pacific Ocean—
Biography. 4. Marine engineers—Texas—Biography.

D767 .R58 2019
940.54/5973092 [B]–dc23
2019027397

*From Texas to Tinian and Tokyo Bay: The Memoirs of Captain J. R. Ritter,
Seabee Commander during the Pacific War, 1942–1945* is Number 17 in the
North Texas Military Biography and Memoir Series

The electronic edition of this book was made possible by the support of the
Vick Family Foundation. Typeset by vPrompt eServices.

# Dedication

**Dedicated to my grandparents, J.R. ("Rex") and Jeannette Catherine Ritter, and to The Seabees of the 107<sup>th</sup> Naval Construction Battalion**

"… The Seabees are the *find* of this war."
—Major General H.W. Smith, USMC (*Can Do!* 23)

"… Without the Seabees the Navy would just be lost in this war."
—Vice-Admiral Thomas C. Kinkaid, USN (*Can Do!* 151)

# Contents

# Chronology of J.R. Ritter's War Years (1941–1946)

**1941**

December 7—Day of Infamy—the Japanese attack Pearl Harbor.

December 8—Applied for a Commission in the Navy Civil Engineer Corps.

December 28—The United States Naval Construction Battalions or the "Seabees" are formed with the authorization of the first naval construction regiment.

**1942**

March 5—All Construction Battalion personnel are officially named "Seabees" by the Navy Department with the creation of the first of the three Seabee battalions.

March 8—Commissioned as Lieutenant, Civil Engineer Corps, U.S. Naval Reserve

April 15—Reported at Camp Allen, Va., for duty.

June 4–6—The Battle of Midway

June 6–7—The Japanese invasion of Attu and Kiska in the Aleutian Islands, the first invasion of American soil in 128 years.

June 5—Left Camp Bradford, Va., with 4th Seabees, for overseas duty.

July 5—Arrived at Dutch Harbor, Alaska, with 4th Seabees.

December—"Spot" promoted to Lieutenant-Commander.

**1943**

March 9—Received orders as Exec. of the 6th Regiment at Adak, Aleutian Islands

March 27—The Battle of the Komandorski Islands.

May 11–30—The Battle of Attu.

May 22—Received orders to report to Camp Peary, Va.

June 18—Reported to Camp Peary (Williamsburg) for duty.

July 17—Orders as OINC (Officer in Charge), 107th Construction Battalion.

July 31—107th Battalion Commissioned by RADM Combs at Camp Endicott, RI.

August 27—The 107<sup>th</sup> Construction Battalion receives orders to transfer to Camp Parks in Pleasanton, California, near Oakland. The 107<sup>th</sup> was stationed in the Bay Area (East Bay) from September–November 1943.

November 7—Married Jeannette Rouyet (1908–1992) in San Francisco.

November 20–23—Battle of Tarawa.

November 22—Reported to ACORN 23 at Port Hueneme.

## 1944

January 31-Feburary 3—The Battle of Kwajalein.

February 20—Received orders for 107<sup>th</sup> to depart Port Hueneme. Flew on one of the Pan Am Clippers from Treasure Island in San Francisco to Pearl Harbor on February 24–25.

March 9—107<sup>th</sup> landed on Ebeye Island in Kwajalein Atoll.

May—Officially promoted to Lieutenant-Commander.

July 24–August 1—The Battle of Tinian.

August 27—Received orders to depart Bigej Island for Tinian, Marianas.

September 12—107<sup>th</sup> arrived in Tinian.

November 24—The first B-29 raid against Japan from the Marianas.

## 1945

April 12—FDR died.

May 8—VE Day—War ended in Europe.

July 22–26—Flew to Australia on B-29 for R&R.

July 30—The heavy cruiser USS *Indianapolis* is sunk by torpedoes from the Japanese submarine *I–58* in the Philippine Sea.

August 6—*Enola Gay* dropped atomic bomb on Hiroshima.

August 9—Second atomic bomb dropped on Nagasaki.

August 14 [VJ Day in the U.S.]—Emperor Hirohito announced unconditional surrender.

August 15—VJ Day—War ended in the Pacific.

September 2—VJ Day—Flew over Tokyo Bay during the signing of the Armistice [the official surrender on the USS *Missouri*].

October—107<sup>th</sup> Battalion deactivated.

November 2—Left Saipan for Home.

November 17—Separation Center - Los Angeles - 90 days Terminal Leave.

November 18—Jeannette met me at San Francisco International Airport.

November 30—Promoted to Commander, CEC, USNR, by Commander Neil Kingsley.

December—Postwar visit to Rosenberg, Texas; New Orleans; East Texas; Austin.

## 1946

January—San Francisco—Looking for a job.

February 12—Terminal Leave ended. Went on "inactive duty" USNR.

# Introduction

T hese are the memoirs of my grandfather, James "Rex" Ritter (1902–1994), a civil engineer from Texas who became a U.S. Navy Seabee officer, about his experiences during World War II in the Aleutians and the Central Pacific from 1942 to 1945. He originally titled it "The War Years, 1941–1946." They include his wartime marriage to my grandmother in San Francisco in 1943, which lasted until her death almost fifty years later. He wrote it from memory as part of his larger memoirs from the 1970s to the 1990s, so they are not a contemporaneous account, but as an engineer he was meticulous and detailed, and his memory was clear to the end of his life. He and my grandmother also preserved primary sources from the war, such as documents, letters, photos, and other items that are in the family collection.

My grandfather, who was called Rex by his family and friends, was born in a small town in East Texas in 1902, where he grew up until he and his family moved to another small town in 1915. He attended the University of Texas, Austin, from 1920 to 1924, where he obtained his degree in civil engineering. While he was a student at the university, in 1920 and 1921, he worked part-time for the Gulf Oil Company, where his father had worked. After he graduated from college he and his best friend rode a motorcycle and sidecar to California, where he was thinking of taking classes at the University of California in Berkeley. The 1920s and 1930s were the era of the great engineering projects, particularly in the western United States, and he was intrigued by the Hetch Hetchy dam and water project in Northern California, a major project that flooded a lovely valley, but which brought clean mountain water to San Francisco, Berkeley, and other cities in the Bay Area. However, he and his friend ran out of money and joined the Merchant Marine from 1924 to 1925, when he made his first visit to San Francisco. He then returned to Texas and worked for the City of Houston Park Department. From 1926 to 1928, he worked for the Roxana Petroleum Corp. From 1928 to 1942, he worked for the Texas State Highway Department and became Assistant District Engineer in Wichita Falls, Texas, in 1935. So, after having had a few jobs after graduating from college, he settled in on a career as a highway engineer. He was fortunate to even have a job even during the Great Depression, but he was a good engineer, it was becoming the age of the automobile, and the State of Texas was building roads to connect its far-flung towns and cities.

By late 1941, as the nation headed toward war, Rex was almost thirty-nine years old and was completing his sixth year as Assistant District Engineer with the Texas State Highway Department in Wichita Falls. His district comprised nine counties, five of which bordered on the Red River and the State of Oklahoma. His primary job was the maintenance of 1,000 miles of state highways in those counties. He was single and was eligible for the draft under the 1940 Selective Service Act (the first peacetime draft in U.S. history).[1] The Texas State Highway Commission had adopted a policy of not asking for deferments for any of their engineers. In any event, by 1941 he wanted to leave Wichita Falls.

Rex was painfully aware that he should try for an officer's commission or end up in the "walking army," as he called it. His new boss offered to help him obtain a commission in the U.S. Army Corps of Engineers; his boss had been a cadet at Texas A&M. Rex asked him to look into it, but nothing happened. During the summer of 1941, Bill Luce, a young ensign in the U.S. Navy Civil

---

1. From 1940 to 1947, over 10,000,000 American men were inducted under the act.

Engineer Corps (CEC), came by Wichita Falls to see his brother Steve, who was one of the engineers in the district and a friend of Rex's. Bill was on his way to Washington, D.C., after a short tour of duty in Alaska. He agreed to send Rex the application forms for a commission in the CEC when he got to Washington, which he did. Rex wrote that he was really busy at that time, so he just stuck the forms in his desk drawer and forgot about them. Like most Americans before Pearl Harbor, Rex knew his life would change, but he did not know how much. There was no military or naval background in his family; he would be the first to serve. It was simply a stroke of luck that he became a naval, rather than an army, engineer.

Before we begin his story, a note to the reader is in order. This is not a history of the Seabees as such, so I will let Rex describe how they were formed and how he came to join them, in his own words, which he does near the beginning of his memoirs. I will, however, give a brief description of the major role they played in the war, which has been often overlooked, especially in the Pacific Campaigns. I believe this oversight was due to the emphasis, both during the war and after, on the combat forces of the U.S. Navy under the celebrated Admirals Chester Nimitz (1885–1966) and William ("Bull") Halsey (1882–1959) in the battles of Midway, Guadalcanal, Leyte Gulf, the Philippine Sea, and Okinawa; the U.S. Army's role under General Douglas MacArthur (1880–1964) in New Guinea and the Philippines; and the heroic actions of the U.S. Marines throughout the Pacific War. (The role of the U.S. Army Air Forces in the Pacific War is usually remembered for the firebombing and the atomic bombings of Japan, which were to play a major part in Rex's memoir by 1945.)

The first three United States Naval Construction Battalions or "Seabees" (a play on words using the letters "c" and "b," symbolized by a fierce-looking bee in a navy uniform, holding both tools and a machine gun) were formed in March 1942. They were organized under the Bureau of Yards and Docks (BUDOCKS), which was one of the eight independent bureaus of the Navy Department.[2] Their duties were to build military facilities and airfields overseas, in both the European and Pacific Theaters.

2. Paul E. Pedisich, *Congress Buys a Navy* (Annapolis: Naval Institute Press, 2016), 17. In 1966 BUDOCKS was renamed the Naval Facilities Engineering Command.

Unlike civilian workers, who would be defenseless if unarmed, or who could be shot as guerrillas if captured and found to be armed, the Seabees were active duty military personnel who were trained to use weapons if necessary and who were entitled to the protections of the Geneva Convention. During World War II, 325,000 men served with the Seabees in 350 units, fighting and building in more than 400 locations by 1945. The enlisted men were generally experienced construction workers, who came from over sixty skilled trades, while the officers were generally experienced civil engineers with construction backgrounds, like Rex. The U.S. Navy Civil Engineer Corps (CEC) had been created in 1867, and nearly 8,000 CEC officers served with the Seabees and commanded their units.[3] In the Pacific Theater, the Seabees built 111 major airstrips, 441 piers, 2258 ammunition magazines, and more.[4] Their slogan was "CAN DO!" Their official motto was *"Construimus, Batuimus,"* which is the Latin for "We build. We fight." (This phrase also incorporates the letters "c" and 'b.") Finally, they were proud to say, "The difficult we do now, the impossible takes a little longer."

Most of the information on the Seabees comes from official U.S. Navy Records. There were two books written during World War II, which I found in my late grandmother's library: *Can Do! The Story of the Seabees* (1944), and *From Omaha to Okinawa: The Story of the Seabees* (1945).[5] They were written by William Bradford Huie, CEC, USNR, a journalist who became a naval officer during the war. Another relevant book, *The Seabees of World War II*, by Edmund L. Castillo, a former naval officer, was published in 1963. This fine book includes a foreword by Admiral Ben Moreell, the wartime Chief of the Bureau of Yards and Docks, who was known as the "Father of the Seabees." I also commend to the reader the "official" *Log of the 107th Seabees, 1943–1945: A Story of a Seabee Battalion conceived in war … Dedicated to peace*, which was

---

3. However, because CEC Officers do not normally exercise command over naval units, Seabee officers were designated as "Officers in Charge" rather than "Commanding Officers."

4. https://www.seabeesmuseum.com/seabee-history  https://web.mst.edu/~rogersda/umrcourses/ge342/SeaBees-Revised.pdf

5. The appendix in *From Omaha to Okinawa* lists 150 Seabee construction battalions and 39 stevedore battalions that were created during the war (221–241).

privately printed in 1945,[6] and the "107th Naval Construction Battalion *Historical Information*," which was provided by the Naval History & Heritage Command.

In 1944 Hollywood made a wartime propaganda film called *The Fighting Seabees* with John Wayne, which my grandfather hated because it misrepresented what the Seabees actually did during the war. At the end of the movie Wayne disobeys orders and gets killed (heroically, of course). Had he lived he would almost certainly have been court-martialed. Rex never disobeyed an order. (He did, however, manage to get them changed, from time to time!) There is, however, one good scene in the movie where a senior naval officer comes up with the term "Seabee" as a play on words, using the abbreviation for "construction battalion."

Finally, a note on how I began this project. My grandfather died when I was still young, so I never had the opportunity to ask him about his wartime experiences. I discovered his typed memoirs after his death in 1994 and began to read them. Although I was interested in his whole life story, I was particularly fascinated by his wartime memoirs, because World War II has always been my special interest as a historian. He wrote clearly and concisely. I have made minor stylistic changes, inserted explanatory footnotes about the Pacific War, the U.S. Navy, and the American home front where necessary, and added an introduction, conclusion, appendices, maps, and references. Otherwise, this is his book, the personal recollections of a naval officer about his experiences in World War II.

This is where his wartime story from 1941 to 1946 begins.

---

6. Baton Rouge, LA: 107th Naval Construction Battalion and Navy Pictorial Publishers, 1946. Digitized version is available online.

# Prologue: December 7, 1941

## *Wichita Falls, Texas*

On Sunday, December 7, 1941, I worked all day in my office alone on budget and finance matters. My phone rang several times but I chose not to be disturbed. Around 5:00 p.m., I finished working in my office and went to the Larson household, where I had rented a room. When I nonchalantly strolled into the Larson living room, the family stared at me. They asked if I had heard the news on the radio. I had not! So they turned the radio on. It was still "blaring out" about the surprise Japanese attack on Pearl Harbor. [The radio was how most Americans found out about Pearl Harbor.] I was so stunned that I said nothing. Instead, I turned on my heels and returned to my office. I feverishly completed the application forms for a commission in the U.S. Navy Civil Engineer Corps. I had previously noted that I did not have the required "proof of birth." I remembered that Mr. Beard, who lived across the road from us when I was born in Murvaul, Texas, was visiting a son in Wichita Falls.

On Monday, December 8, our government declared war on Japan.[1] During the day, I took "Sally" Waters, the boss' secretary and also a notary, out to the Beard home. We obtained a notarized statement from Mr. Beard as proof of my birth. Later in the day I mailed my application papers to Washington, D.C.

1. In San Francisco, my grandmother Jeannette Rouyet and her class listened to FDR's famous Pearl Harbor speech to Congress on the radio in the auditorium of Aptos Junior High School (now Aptos Middle School). On the 65th anniversary of Pearl Harbor, the writer and historian Carl Nolte described how the attack impacted and changed San Francisco in "San Francisco: Pearl Harbor was a close thing for the city in 1941." (*San Francisco Chronicle*, December 7, 2006). My grandmother remembered having heard false rumors of Japanese airplanes heading toward San Francisco in December 1941, when the West Coast was jittery after Pearl Harbor.

# Chapter 1

✦

✦

✦

✦

✦

# 1942: Texas to the Aleutians

## Training for the Seabees

Early in January 1942, Cmdr. John Perry, Personnel Officer in the Bureau of Yards & Docks, Washington, D.C., sent me an offer of a commission as lieutenant, Civil Engineer Corps, U.S. Navy. I thought I qualified for lieutenant commander[1]; however, I doubted that I had time to negotiate even though Commander Perry was another Texan from Waco. I immediately indicated my acceptance of lieutenant's rank. Later I received my commission, with date and rank of March 8, 1942. Now I was a full-fledged officer in the naval reserves, subject for call to active duty at any time. Late in 1941, I traded in my 1936 Pontiac for a new 1941 Buick Special. The Pontiac had been a real "lemon" and this new green Buick Special was my pride and joy. However, I was not sure how long I would be able to enjoy it.[2]

After I received and accepted my naval reserve commission, my boss Mr. Isbell relieved me of my Assistant District Engineer duties. He placed me in charge of completing an "access" road to

1. A glossary of US Navy Commissioned Officer ranks is given in the Appendix.
2. No new cars were made in the U.S. during the war from 1942–1945.

Sheppard Field, an Army Air Corps[3] base just north of the city limits of Wichita Falls. This was an interesting but short-lived job. It involved an overpass over the Fort Worth & Denver Railroad and a four-lane paved road to the air base. It was good to be back in construction again, particularly since I had had little support in my assistant duties. This new job was more relaxing and moved swiftly. It had all the "push" the federal government could muster to complete in short order.

On April 10, 1942, I received a telegram from the navy comman-dant in New Orleans to report to NOB [Naval Operating Base] Norfolk, Virginia, by April 15. After seven years in Wichita Falls, I had to leave in three days in order to go to Dallas for my navy "physical" and to Rosenberg [Texas] to say goodbye to my parents and leave my Buick Special with my dad. My stay in Wichita Falls had been interesting from a professional standpoint. My fourteen years' experience with the Texas State Highway Department, I thought, should come in handy as a Civil Engineer Corps officer in the navy. I left Wichita Falls with no regrets, except that I would miss the Larsons, with whom I had enjoyed many pleasant expe-riences during my stay in their home. We called them "Mom" & "Pop." "Pop" worked for the Fort Worth & Denver Railroad in Fort Worth and came home on weekends. Earlier, he was a switch-man in Wichita Falls, where he lost a leg in a switching accident. He was fitted with an artificial limb and had an office job in Fort Worth. He and mom loved to go dancing. He could dance better than I could, even with the artificial limb. I often had dinner at the Larsons and still remember fondly the fried chicken. I gave the family a fond farewell and headed out with all my earthly posses-sions in my new Buick for Dallas.

## *Dallas and Rosenberg, Texas*

As I drove into Dallas, I remembered fondly the many pleasant weekends I had enjoyed in this city as a respite from dull Wichita Falls. I reflected on the "Opera under the Stars" in the fairgrounds and the pleasant times in the old Adolphus Hotel. With Dallas, Oklahoma City, and Fort Worth as escapes from Wichita Falls, life was bearable.

3. The Army Air Corps became the U.S. Army Air Forces (USAAF) in June 1941.

I reported to the medical officer in the naval reserve office in Dallas. He informed me that I had such a heavy cold that he could not pass me in my physical. He advised that I return to Wichita Falls and report back to him when I had recovered. I informed him that I could not return there since I had "pulled stakes" and besides, I had telegraphed orders to report to Norfolk. I pleaded with him to forget about my heavy cold, give me some medication, and let me pass my physical exam. To my surprise and delight, he did just that. Next morning, I headed south for my parents' home in Rosenberg.

I only had an overnight stay with my folks and saw my brother and sister. I persuaded my dad to take charge of my new Buick and promised to come back for it as soon as the indoctrination period was over in Norfolk. I expected to be sent to either New Orleans or Corpus Christi for duty.

## Norfolk and Camp Allen (Naval Operating Base), Virginia

My train from Houston arrived in Norfolk, Virginia, on April 15, 1942. I went immediately to NOB Norfolk to report in compliance with the telegraphic orders. Here, the officer-of -the-day told me I should report to Camp Allen (Naval Construction Training Center), which was on the outskirts of the naval operating base.

At 1820 (6:20 p.m.) on April 15, I reported to Capt. Ware, commanding officer, NCTC, Camp Allen, for duty. I was assigned quarters in the Bachelor Officers' Quarters (BOQ) on the base and was told to report for duty the following morning. I missed supper at the officers' mess and then went directly to the BOQ. This building was still under construction and the windows of my quarters had not been installed. Although the heat was on in the building, it was quite cold in the room assigned to me. I wandered around the BOQ and located the wardroom. Here I was greeted and welcomed aboard by two other Civil Engineer Corps lieutenants who had reported for initial duty two weeks earlier.

Lieutenant Peppin was from San Francisco and a graduate in architecture from the University of California. He had worked for several years for Standard Oil in San Francisco, designing and building company filling stations. He was surprised he had been accepted to the Civil Engineer Corps since he was an architect and not a civil engineer. Lt. Cooper was from Mississippi and had been running a large farm there, rather than practicing engineering for which he had been trained. He told me he was anxious to get this war over as soon as possible so he could get back to his farm. I somehow felt this would take a little longer than he anticipated.

Both of these officers seemed pleased to have me report, since they envisioned some relief from O.D. (Officer-of-the-Day) duties they had been stuck with since their arrival. Since I did not have a navy uniform yet, I expressed doubt that I would be assigned to duty officer duties and would probably not yet afford them immediate relief. I surmised from their comments that the duty officer assignment was a disagreeable chore.

After our lengthy "bull session" in the ward room, I returned to my cold quarters to get some rest. It had been a long but interesting day. It was a miserable first night in the cold room and not enough covers. Next morning I went to breakfast at the officers' mess. After missing supper last night, I was quite hungry. I had my first introduction to navy beans for breakfast; however, the coffee was excellent. Now I was ready to embark on my new duties. I reported to Captain Ware's staff and was introduced to Cmdr. Harry Bolles, Executive Officer, and Lt. Cmdr. Howard Ransford, training officer. Commander Bolles was a fine-looking officer with a pleasing personality. Lieutenant-Commander Ransford was a small fellow, about 145 pounds, but reflected a quiet efficiency. Both were U.S. Naval Academy graduates and Civil Engineer Corps officers. The "Skipper," Captain Ware, was a "Line" officer, with earlier duty on destroyers.[4]

I remembered Lieutenant Commander Ransford as the famous Naval Academy quarterback with the nickname of "Shag." Several years before, while in school, he piloted the navy team to come from behind and tie the army team at Soldier's Field in Chicago, 21 to 21. He was quite a hero to all the old navy grads. "Shag" gave me some material to read and study and advised me to return as "Duty Officer" that evening. I explained to him that that I had been called to active duty on short notice and did not have the time to

4. In the US Navy, "line" officers exercise command authority, as opposed to "staff" officers, whose authority is more limited. The term dates from the 18th century, when officers of the Royal Navy commanded "ships of the line." See Paul E. Pedisich, *Congress Buys a Navy*, 19–20.

procure a navy uniform, therefore I would probably not be eligible for the duty. He inferred that this made no difference, since they were short on officers for this duty and I could perform in civilian clothes. He advised that a chief petty officer would be on hand to "show me the ropes." It would appear that the navy wasted no time in getting me into harness, despite the lack of a uniform.

On my first day of duty at this naval construction training center, I took the material Lieutenant Commander Ransford had given me to peruse back to the officer's ward room. From a brief study of the material, I became aware of why I had been called to active duty. I was here at Camp Allen to be trained as a Civil Engineer Corps officer for assignment to a construction battalion (the "Seabees") for overseas duty in the war zone. This was the first time that I was aware of the existence of construction battalions. I had envisioned being assigned to a shore station in Public Works near my home in Texas. I had hoped for duty either in New Orleans or Corpus Christi. It appeared that I could forget about my new Buick that I had left with my dad for the unforeseeable future.

All this came as a rude shock to a fresh-caught navy lieutenant who did not even own a uniform. My first thought was to stick around for a while and hope for a transfer to a shore station in the continental USA. Or, I might even consider resigning my commission and returning to the Texas State Highway Department. Surely, my services back there would be useful to national defense in building and maintaining roads and streets for military use. As I mused on these ideas, I suddenly became reconciled to the fact that I really had no such choice. I was stuck with the "Seabees," so I might as well accept that fact, and proceed to familiarize myself with construction battalion objectives.

I found the background and origin of construction battalions in the navy very interesting. The idea had sprung from the fertile mind of Rear Adm. Ben Moreell, Chief of Civil Engineers and Chief of the Bureau of Yards & Docks, Washington, D.C. He had been selected earlier for this job by President Franklin Roosevelt himself. He came directly from the rank of commander and never really served as captain. Historically, civilian construction companies had been used to build naval installations and civilians were used to perform necessary maintenance at shore establishments. Right after Pearl Harbor it became painfully apparent that contractors would have difficulty recruiting and keeping civilian workers in war zones. If they armed them for their own protection or to defend their installations, they would be classified as guerrillas and could be shot by the enemy in lieu of becoming prisoners of war. This was vividly illustrated during the Battle of Midway Island in June 1942, where civilians working on navy contracts had to be evacuated.

Ben Moreell persuaded Congress to authorize the formation of naval construction battalions. Then he set out to recruit officers and enlisted men from civilian life. I was one of these. He placed trained construction men in uniform, with the support of the building trades unions throughout the country. He gave ranks to the officers recruited and rates to the enlisted men, commensurate with their experience in civilian pursuits. In order to insure union support, he pledged not to use naval construction battalions for the construction of facilities within the continental USA. In line with this verbal assurance, he was able to recruit builders with "know-how." Since they would be in a military uniform, they would be able to defend themselves as well as protect their installations. This program was an immediate success, being able to recruit patriotic and experienced construction men for overseas military construction.

For several days after I reported to NCTC at Camp Allen, I served as Officer-of-the-Day (Duty Officer) in civilian clothes. Fortunately, there was an experienced chief petty officer (chief yeoman) to tell me what to do. This "fresh caught" officer certainly did not know what to do. In a short time, with his assistance, I found out how to "run the desk." Incidentally, the officer-of-the-day is the same position ashore that the officer-of-the-deck is aboard a navy ship. This is the reception and information center for the command. All inquiries concerning the command come through this office. Visitors to see the commanding officer or executive officer clear through the duty officer. Officers and men leaving or returning to the base log in and out with that officer. One learns a lot in a short period of time about the command and its operation. This is the "nerve center" of the command. I felt quite conspicuous sitting behind a desk, performing military duties in civilian clothes.

Newly recruited officers were prime targets for the assignment to the "duty" desk, which had to be manned 24 hours a day, due to a shortage of officers available for this job. Also, after a relatively short period, newly reporting officers were assigned to battalions being formed. The primary function of this command was to form construction battalions and get them into the field (war zone) as quickly as possible, since they were in urgent demand overseas, due to the fast- moving war situation. The command had to work feverishly to comply with deadlines set by the Navy Department in Washington. Battalion activation and dispatch were the prime functions of this base.

After about a week of this hectic rat-race in the duty office, I got up the nerve to go and see the executive officer, Commander Bolles, to request a day off to go into downtown Norfolk to procure a uniform. He immediately gave me permission and chided me for not asking sooner. The supply officer at the base gave me the detailed list of items that I must obtain to qualify for the uniform gratuity of $250. An extraneous item was a sword belt. Due to the steel short-age, Congress had deleted the requirement for an officer's sword, but forgot to delete the sword belt. The supply officer agreed that the item of the belt was superfluous, but if I wanted the gratuity, I had better get it. In Norfolk I went down to Frank Thomas, an old established uniform shop that served the naval officers in this area for years. I obtained the complete outfit, including the sword belt, to conform to the uniform allowance. Since I had not received the gratuity or any pay from the navy yet, Frank Thomas graciously agreed to charge the bill to my account. Now, for the first time since reporting for active duty, I was able to don a naval uniform for the rank of lieutenant.

That evening, I reported to the duty desk in uniform for the first time. After midnight, the shore patrol brought in a drunken sailor from downtown Norfolk. Normally, I would have had the chief on duty take him to his quarters and put him to bed in his bunk; however, this sailor had gotten into a fight, resisted a civilian police officer, and damaged property in a bar. The shore patrol had rescued him from the civilian authorities in Norfolk and returned him to the base to face charges. The sailor was still in a belligerent mood, so I had no choice but to have him confined to the brig [navy prison] for safe keeping. With the help of the duty chief, I wrote up the charges for the use of Captain Ware at Captain's Mast at 0900 the same morning. "Captain's Mast" is a one-man court where the commanding officer may give limited punishments for minor offenses. Early in the morning, I personally delivered the charges to the captain's yeoman. The captain arrived on time to handle some twenty culprits, including our drunken sailor. I was present, as required, to substantiate the written report. However, when the culprit came before the captain, they could not find my report. The captain told me I had failed in my duty in bringing in a prisoner without written charges. When I explained I had prepared the report and given it to his personal yeoman, he reminded me that it was my job as duty officer to see that the charges were in his hand for the mast. To my disgust, he released our prisoner. Later, when I tried to explain the situation to Lieutenant Commander Ransford, the training officer, I got no sympathy. He only reminded me not to let this happen again. My initial reaction was "Aw, to hell with the navy!" but I had learned a valuable lesson on the navy requirement to always "follow through."

The skipper, Capt. Jimmie Ware, a line officer, was in a shore assignment as C.O. at Camp Allen. According to navy "scuttlebutt" (rumor), he had disobeyed orders during a training exercise one foggy night on the West Coast. He was the C.O. of a destroyer following the lead ship when he sensed trouble and made an unauthorized right turn. The lead ship crashed into rocks on the shore line with loss of lives and the ship. Commander Ware was reprimanded for disobeying orders, although he saved his ship, and was not given another sea command. It was said that he would never be made admiral due to this incident. The navy is a hard taskmaster![5]

As commanding officer of this navy base, Captain Ware was responsible for activating the early construction battalions. The 1st Battalion had been activated before I arrived at Camp Allen. It was dispatched quickly and sent out in separate companies attached to a [U.S.] Marine regiment. This group had the nickname of "Bobcats" and went to the South Pacific. They were with the

5. The incident that cost Captain Ware his sea command was probably the Honda Point disaster of 1923, in which nine destroyers ran aground on the coast near Santa Barbara and 23 sailors died. The largest peacetime loss of ships in the history of the U.S. Navy, it is described in the book *Tragedy at Honda* (Annapolis, MD: Naval Institute Press, 2012; originally published in 1960). In an eerie foreshadowing of the Pacific War against Japan almost 20 years later, part of the cause of the disaster was the Great Tokyo Earthquake of 1923 that had occurred one week before, which set off a giant tsunami that caused unusual currents off the California coast.

marines on the assaults at such places as Guadalcanal [1942–1943]. The 2nd Battalion had also departed before I arrived. This unit was split into two groups. One group went to Pearl Harbor and the other to the South Pacific attached to the marines.

The 3rd Battalion was in the process of being activated when I arrived at Camp Allen. My earliest associates on my arrival, Lieutenants Cooper and Peppin, were assigned to the Third. I was also tentatively assigned to the 3rd Battalion, but it was never formed. I saw my friends boarding a troop train heading for Port Hueneme, California. This was a Seabee base near Oxnard, 40 miles up the coast from Los Angeles. This was the final training and embarkation base for construction battalions going into the Pacific war zones. On arrival here, the Third was divided into separate companies and sent to join various marine units in the South Pacific.

The 4th Battalion was in the process of being activated; however, their officer complement was filled, so it would appear I missed this one also. In the meantime, I was given various assignments under Lieutenant Commander Ransford, the training officer at the base. I enjoyed working with "Shag," as he was called; however, I made it clear to him that I did not wish to remain indefinitely at Camp Allen. Soon I was given an officer assignment in the Fifth Battalion now being activated. Before I reported to the officer-in-charge of the Fifth, "Shag" told me that he had persuaded the company commander of Company A in the Fourth to remain at the base as his assistant training officer. This billet was now open in the Fourth. I went to see the officer-in-charge of the Fourth Battalion, and he immediately accepted me as the new Company A commander.

The "skipper" of the Fourth Construction Battalion was Lt. Cmdr. Joe Bronson from Walnut Creek, California, across the Bay from San Francisco [where my grandfather later went in 1943]. He was originally from Columbus, Ohio, and was a graduate Civil Engineer from Ohio State. He had wide experience in heavy construction and waterfront work in the San Francisco Bay Area and Hawaii. He also had a wife and four children back in Walnut Creek. I was impressed with his background, personality and natural leadership, and was happy to accept the billet as one of his five company commanders. His executive officer was Lt. Neil Kingsley, a Naval Academy graduate with a masters in civil engineering from RPI (Rensselaer Polytechnic Institute) on the Hudson River at Troy, New York. It was good to have a trained professional from the Naval Academy as our executive officer, especially since I was strictly unmilitary. Three of the four company commanders were Texans—Lt. (j.g) Ordis Forbess had Company B and Lt. (j.g) Clark Stroud had Company D. Forbess had gone to Texas Tech and Stroud had worked in the Texas State Highway Department, so I felt quite at home in this battalion.

A standard construction battalion had a quota of 33 officers and 1,030 enlisted men. There was an officer-in-charge, executive officer, captain, two medical officers, one dental officer, two supply officers (one in commissary), headquarters company commander (design, security, housing, subsistence and fiscal), and four construction companies to build and maintain advance base facilities. I was company commander of one of the four construction companies with junior officers, warrant officers, chief petty officers, 1st, 2nd & 3rd class petty officers, and 1st and 2nd class seamen.

We were quite busy completing our personnel quotas, getting to know our junior officers and enlisted men, and familiarizing ourselves with the types of jobs we might be called on to perform. We utilized marine personnel to train us in necessary military functions. We had a hectic pace during this organizational period of the battalion. We would be leaving Camp Allen on the completion of filling our battalion complement. The fully activated' 4th Construction Battalion would move to Camp Bradford, an advance base camp fifteen miles away on the Atlantic Coast near Virginia Beach. Here we would be on our own, including providing subsistence and security and our own training program. After a short period here, we would move to Port Hueneme, California, as our final advance base prior to sailing to the war zone in the South Pacific.

On the day prior to our leaving Camp Allen for Camp Bradford, Lieutenant Kingsley, our exec, and I were walking back to the battalion office when suddenly I spied my old friend, Howard Pipkin, in a chief's uniform, walking alone. Before I left Texas, I knew he had enlisted in the naval reserve as a chief carpenter's mate (surveyor). Later, he was called to active duty from his home in Fort Worth and ordered to Great Lakes Training Center, near Chicago, for boot training. He had just arrived at Camp Allen for further training and assignment to a construction battalion. After introducing "Pip" to Lieutenant Kingsley, I suggested that he would be very useful in the Fourth if we still had a vacancy in his rate as CPO. Our executive readily agreed and asked "Pip" to come along with us to see our skipper about adding him to our roster. "Pip" demurred, stating that he had just arrived and was scheduled to enter a training program at Camp Allen. Kingsley and I both assured him that he would not miss anything by joining up with us. Our skipper, Joe Bronson, was delighted to offer "Pip" a billet in our battalion due to his extensive background in highway design and construction.

Incidentally, I first met "Pip" in Waco in 1930 where we worked as project engineers in a highway residency. Later, he joined me at Wichita Falls as a resident engineer with the Texas State Highway Department. Later he transferred to Fort Worth, where he was in charge of expressways in that city, also as resident engineer with the highway department. Our skipper agreed that we were lucky indeed to find this chief with such an extensive background and all the qualifications of an officer. However, he felt that due to our long association in civilian life, it might be awkward for "Pip" to be in Co. A with me—so he was assigned to Co. D with Lt. (j.g.) Clark Stroud. He had also been with the Highway Department in Abilene, Texas, before reporting for active duty—so this was a "natural" for "Pip" to be in Stroud's unit. Needless to say, I was delighted with this turn of events.

## Camp Bradford, Virginia

At Camp Bradford, the 4th Construction Battalion became a self-sufficient organization. We were all alone and had to fend for ourselves. We no longer had the staff at Camp Allen to lean on and go to for advice and help. Here, we were housed by companies in Quonset huts,[6] maintained our own subsistence and messing.

6. A Quonset hut is a lightweight prefab built of corrugated galvanized steel having a semicircular cross-section. The American design was based on the Nissen hut introduced by the British during World War I. "A production facility was quickly set up by George A. Fuller and Co. in West Davisville, not far from the Davisville Naval Base. Capt. Raymond V. Miller, CEC, USN, had concerns about patent issues with Great Britain if they used the name Nissen Hut. Since the

We also performed our own training with our battalion personnel, including advance base building (Quonset huts), equipment operation and military (including use of rifle and pistol ranges).

We knew that our stay here would be brief so we worked furiously to firm up our company organizations and job selection for our personnel. This might just be our last chance for real advance base training before going overseas into the war zone. We would leave here shortly for Port Hueneme for transshipment to an overseas advance base.

In spite of long hours in this hectic "rat-race," I managed to get a little rest and recreation. I spent a delightful weekend at a fine resort hotel at Virginia Beach nearby. This resort was located in a pine grove with a small lake, dogwoods in bloom, and an ocean beach adjacent for swimming. There was also a small golf course, but I did not get to play. I also spent one night at Old Point Comfort in another resort hotel, where I met Marge Bronson, the skipper's wife and Mrs. Raig Bigger, wife of our senior medical officer. Also, there were other officers' wives staying there to be close to their husbands before they left for overseas. I had a very pleasant evening there.

On May 29, 1942 we received orders to prepare to depart for Port Hueneme. This is what we had been waiting for. We had all worked furiously, with no leaves to get everything ready for imminent departure for the West Coast.

## En Route to Port Hueneme

On June 5, 1942 [as the Battle of Midway was taking place in the Pacific], we were ordered to depart for the Seabee Training Center at Port Hueneme, California, on the Pacific Coast north of Los Angeles. We boarded three all-Pullman trains at the station adjacent to Camp Bradford. The skipper was on Train #1, accompanied by Dr. Bigger, the senior medical officer. The Company C commander was in charge of Train #2, with the junior medical officer to provide any needed medical assistance while en route. I was train commander on Train #3, with the dental officer aboard

area was known as Quonset Point (the word Quonset means "boundary" in the language of the Native American Narragansett people who once lived on the land), the new design was called a "Quonset Hut." https://www.seabeesmuseum.com/visit/quonset-huts

to act as our medical officer while en route. We also had a couple of hospital corpsmen assigned to my train.

I was in charge of this train and responsible for all personnel, comprising one-third of the battalion complement. The railroad train conductor reported to me; however, he was in charge of train operation. I had a stateroom near the head of the train, which also served as my office. I organized the officers aboard my section with duties such as security, military conduct, messing, etc. It was up to me to run a taut ship and see that we arrived safely at our destination. This was a secret troop movement, with secret orders. No one was to contact friends or relatives en route since that might violate our safety or endanger our personnel. This prohibition could well present a problem, since our route could take us by the home towns of many of our people.

We pulled out of the train yard at Camp Bradford over the Southern Railway Line. Everyone was in a happy mood, since this is why we came on active duty in the first place. Now, we were en route to fulfill our mission. This was the beginning of the real thing.

Our train rolled on smoothly and without incident through the Carolinas. We stopped briefly at a small town south of Columbus. The parents of a young ensign on our train were on hand to greet their son. This was the first incidence of a break in our security. Our ensign feigned surprise that his parents would know he was on this train. It was obvious that somehow word had gotten out to a trainman, who had alerted the young officer's parents. After we pulled out of the town, I sent for the ensign and gave him a stern lecture regarding officers, who of all people should be the last to leak information about secret [wartime] troop train movements.

Just after passing Macon, Georgia, our train came to a violent stop. The conductor came for me and asked me to accompany him to the front of our train. There had been an accident, which I should be aware of. He explained that a man had been run over by our train. As train commander it was my unpleasant duty to witness what had happened. This was a gruesome sight. A small man with a red beard had been run over by the wheel of a coach car which cut his body in half. The conductor surmised that he was a hobo trying to board our train for a free ride, lost his footing and fell between two cars. After some delay to remove the body and report the incident to local authorities, we were allowed to proceed. I had a couple of sleepless nights as I relived the sight of this unfortunate accident involving the life of another human being. Here we were en route to the war zone where people were dying, but not by accident.

As we continued southward, I was aware that we were passing through the home country of many of our personnel. We had to maintain tight security to forestall the temptation on the part of some enlisted men to leave the train and return home. No one did this; however, we had a couple of incidents when we passed through Alabama and Mississippi where relatives were at the depot to meet the train. In each instance, we arranged to have the relatives go inside the depot and allowed one of our guards to accompany their son for a brief visit out of sight of our other personnel.

We passed through Shreveport, Louisiana, which is only 50 miles from where I grew up on a farm in East Texas. I was not tempted to leave the train and phone relatives. At Marshall, Texas, we were switched out of the I. & G.N. (International and Great Northern Railway) and proceeded through Texas past Austin and San Antonio. I was in familiar territory as I looked out my stateroom window.

At San Antonio we switched to the Southern Pacific lines, with which we would stay until Los Angeles, or perhaps Oxnard, which is six miles from Port Hueneme. As we changed railroad lines, we kept our original Pullman cars and changed only the engine and train crews. During our train trip, we maintained our own small store for the purchase of cigarettes, candy, soft drinks and sundries. At designated stops, a chief petty officer and several enlisted men were detailed to leave the train to replenish our supplies for the small store from the station restaurant. A storekeeper from the Supply Department ran the small store on a non-profit basis.

After leaving San Antonio, our train made a stop at Del Rio, which is on the Rio Grande. Mexico is just across the river. At Del Rio I forbade anyone to go ashore or allow an outsider aboard our train, for I knew that booze could be easily smuggled aboard at this notoriously wet town. I told the chief in charge of the small store that they could replenish their stock at Sanderson, 40 miles west. I remembered that Sanderson was dry territory. Although this ruse was designed to thwart some of these old construction men from obtaining liquor, I did not reckon with the cleverness of some of my drinking Seabees. Someone passed the word out the train window at Del Rio that we would have a detail go ashore at Sanderson. A liquor merchant evidently made the trip by car with a load of booze and arranged for it to be brought on the train with the other supplies. I was not aware of what had happened until I noted that we were dealing with some rowdy drunks all the way to El Paso. Unfortunately, one of those imbibing freely was one of our sentries on duty between cars. Since being drunk on sentry duty is a grave offense and cannot be tolerated, I held captain's mast on the culprit and deprived him of any shore leave at our next shore base. By the time we reached El Paso, everything quieted down, so I assumed that all the liquor brought aboard at Sanderson had been consumed. Since most of my Seabees were ex-construction men, I should have expected they would find a way to get a drink. Which reminds me of one construction man's observation to another: "Here it is Saturday night, so I gotta get drunk and I sure do dread it."

Another train crew came on in El Paso, which would be with us all the way to Los Angeles. The new conductor reported to me as train commander to tell me he would take us into Los Angeles, and from there we would continue on to Seattle. I told him my basic orders stated that we would continue from Los Angeles to Port Hueneme. However, for some reason, I believed the conductor had information I did not possess. I swore the commander to secrecy regarding the Seattle destination and did not reveal this information to any of the officers or men. I decided to await our arrival in Los Angeles to check out the conductor's story. As we rode along the countryside through New Mexico, Arizona and Southern California, I would look out the window of my stateroom and remember scenes from an earlier trip back in 1924 on my motorcycle en route to Los Angeles. This was a much more pleasant way to travel—and at government expense.

## Los Angeles

Our train arrived in Los Angeles early in the morning of June 12, 1942. We stopped at a train yard in the outskirts of the city. Now I would be able to check out the conductor's story regarding our going on to Seattle rather than Port Hueneme. I went down to the yardmaster's office and got in touch with my skipper, Lieutenant

Commander Bronson, by phone. His train was in another part of this train yard. I informed him regarding our conductor's word regarding our proceeding on to Seattle. The skipper said he believed the conductor might have information that we did not have, since his conductor had told him the same story. He had already placed a call to Cmdr. John Perry in Washington, D.C. for verification. He asked me to stand by the phone until he called me back. Shortly thereafter, he called me back to advise me that he had telephone orders for the battalion to proceed to Puget Sound Naval Shipyard, which is just across the sound from Seattle. So the "scuttlebutt" from our train conductor proved to be a real thing.

After I found out that we would not be going to Port Hueneme after all [where the 107th Seabees would later be stationed in 1943–1944], I returned to my quarters on our train and called the officers together to report the change in our plans. We would be leaving shortly on the same train for Seattle. Only one officer in my group expressed any qualms about this change in our plans. He was Ensign Booth from headquarters' company. He was from Los Angeles and had attended Cal Tech there. He had looked forward to a visit with his folks. Now, due to the secret nature of our travel on this troop train, he would not be permitted to phone his parents. He was very tall and when he rose he almost bumped the ceiling of my stateroom. Then he exclaimed: "Lieutenant Ritter, do you mean to tell us that you are going to violate our basic written orders and move on to Seattle on just a telephone call?" I answered; "Yes, Mr. Booth, that is what I intend to do. Just what would you do under these circumstances?" As he sat down, he was almost in tears, but replied: "I guess I would do just what you are doing—take us on to Seattle."

The officers then silently left my stateroom to carry out their assignments preparatory to our moving out of Los Angeles railway yard. Just before noon, on the same day as our arrival, we left the Los Angeles area and headed north on the Southern Pacific Lines en route to Seattle.

## En Route to Seattle

As our train pulled out, I could not help but feel sorry for Mr. Booth and other personnel on our train from this area. However, this was just another lesson in reconciliation to military necessity. For some

reason, not known to me at this time, the Navy Department had
decided to change our destination and mission. We had received
news that a few days earlier, the Japanese had bombed Dutch
Harbor [on June 3, 1942, just before the Battle of Midway began]
on the Aleutian chain in Alaska.[7] Perhaps we might be headed in
that direction instead of the South Pacific.

We had a pleasant train ride through California, past Sacramento and through the Cascades into Oregon. The scenery through
Oregon was magnificent. Evidently our men from Southern California
had become reconciled [to not stopping in Los Angeles], and
everything went smoothly. Just a short distance out of Portland,
however, one of our enlisted men became quite ill rather suddenly.
Although our medical officer on our train was the battalion dental
commander, he arose to the occasion and diagnosed the illness
as appendicitis. Between us, we had to make a quick decision.
Should we transfer him to a hospital in Portland or take the risk of
taking him with us to Seattle? The dentist and I decided it was not
worth the risk of taking him on to Seattle, so I got the conductor to
arrange for an ambulance to meet our train in Portland. When we
arrived, the ambulance was on hand and took him to the marine
hospital. The wisdom of our decision to leave him in Portland was
confirmed when he joined us later in Puget Sound. His appendix
was on the verge of bursting, so he probably would have been dead
on our arrival in Seattle. Just another one of the joys of being train
commander!

Our train arrived in Seattle early on June 15, 1942 [at King
Street Station, which was the transportation hub of Seattle in the
1940s]. We were immediately transferred to a ferry for the ride
across Puget Sound to the shipyard. The ferry ride was pleasant,
with beautiful scenery on all sides. It was great to see familiar
scenes that I had witnessed back in 1925 as a sailor in the Merchant

7. The Japanese invaded the Aleutian islands of Kiska and Attu on June 6–7,
1942, the first foreign invasion of U.S. soil since the War of 1812. The Aleutian
Islands Campaign in 1942–1943 is known as the "Forgotten Battle" of the Pacific
War, due to its being overshadowed by the simultaneous and more famous
Guadalcanal Campaign in the South Pacific. The Americans were concerned that
the Japanese would use the Aleutians as a launching pad to bomb Seattle and
San Francisco. See Simon Rigge and the Editors of Time-Life Books, War in the
Outposts (Alexandria, VA: Time-Life Books,World War II Series, 1980), 125–128.

Marine on the good ship *Vinita*. We had quite a train ride for 10 days since leaving Camp Bradford, Virginia. Despite the responsibility for the personnel on my train, I had really enjoyed the circuitous route across the United States. We really had good food in the dining car. Now I could look forward to rejoining the rest of the Fourth Seabees at the Puget Sound Naval Shipyard.

## Puget Sound Naval Shipyard

This base is located across the Puget Sound from Seattle. It is on a beautiful island. We reported here on June 15, 1942, and received our written modified orders. We would be quartered here and outfitted, awaiting first available transportation to Dutch Harbor in the Aleutian Islands, Territory of Alaska.

The 4th Construction Battalion was back together again under our regular military organization. We were quartered in large wooden barracks by companies. My main job was looking out for the needs of Company A and being sure we complied with base regulations. Since we were messed at the base cafeteria, we were spared having to provide this function. Therefore we were able to devote most of our time putting our organization together to be able to perform our assignments when we reached Dutch Harbor. Hopefully, we would be outfitted here with materials and equipment to enable us to adequately perform our mission at Dutch Harbor.

The base at Dutch Harbor had been in the process of being expanded by a civilian contractor, which was standard procedure in the Navy Department. However, the bombing by the Japanese had frightened the civilian workers, and they were leaving the place in great numbers—depending on sea transportation back to Seattle. The 4th Seabees were ordered to the rescue to assure completion of needed expansions at Dutch Harbor.

There really wasn't much to do at Puget Sound, so I would frequently take a ferry over to Seattle[8] during the evenings to have dinner and catch a show. Two weeks after our arrival here, we received orders for the battalion to report to the commanding officer of the USS *Grant* for transportation to Dutch Harbor.

8. In the 1940s, Seattle was a small Pacific Northwest city that was known mostly for being the home of Boeing, before the 1962 World's Fair or Century 21 Fair put the city on the world map.

We had hoped to receive construction equipment normally assigned to a Seabee battalion here at Puget Sound, so we could be assured of performing our mission on arrival at Dutch Harbor. However, we were told that the civilian contractor at Dutch Harbor had enough on hand to satisfy our requirements. Our skipper had tried to convince DIRALDOCKS (Director, Alaskan Division, Bureau of Yards and Docks) in Seattle that we should leave here with our equipment to insure our ability to perform our mission. The captain in charge was adamant, insisting the civilian contractor could take care of us in that department. It was obvious this "old line" CEC Captain was not sympathetic to the new Seabee idea of navy construction, and resisted any change in the way of doing navy work with civilian contracts. We found out all too soon that we had been "short-changed" in Seattle.

## En Route to Dutch Harbor

On June 29, 1942, we loaded our personnel, supplies, materials and a few scanty pieces of equipment aboard the USS *Grant* for our sea voyage to Dutch Harbor, Alaska. The 4th Seabees had the good fortune to be the first battalion to leave on a mission intact. Other battalions had been broken up in units and dispersed with marine battalions. The 4th Battalion was making history in this regard. Despite our equipment debacle, we felt good about leaving on a mission with a full battalion. We were really making history.

The USS *Grant* was part of a fleet of cruise ships owned by the American President Lines out of San Francisco. It was now under charter to the navy as a troop ship. Since the Japanese attack on Pearl Harbor, all ships leaving Seattle for Alaskan bases sailed by way of Vancouver, British Columbia, and then along the Inside Passage, close up the Alaskan coast to Kodiak, and then to the Aleutian chain. This precaution was taken due to the suspected presence of Japanese submarines in the Pacific. Our ship was selected to be the first to sail out of Puget Sound directly to Dutch Harbor. Ostensibly, this was done to hasten our arrival there. Due to submarine hazards, we had frequent fire and boat drills and carried life jackets with us at all times. We had several alarms, but fortunately they were false. Most of us were frightened at the prospects of having to hit the cold water there if our ship was sunk. We were told that no one could survive more than 30 minutes.

Skipper Joe Bronson kept us busy interviewing each chief petty officer in our company and required a written report on each one's qualifications. This kept my officers and me busy and ensured our familiarity with our chiefs' potential. Our skipper later admitted that he did not read the reports, but thought we had gained by the procedure. A few of my Seabees got seasick en route, but I made it fine, probably due to my earlier experiences in the Merchant Marine.

## Dutch Harbor, Alaska

On July 5, 1942, the USS *Grant* sailed into Dutch Harbor and docked at Ballyhoo Docks, in the shadow of a bare and forbidding mountain, Mount Ballyhoo. The whole area was treeless and had a desolate and forbidding appearance. This island is relatively small, but has been a navy base since our acquisition of Alaska from the Russians in 1867. Just across a narrow channel is Unalaska, a much larger island with rugged terrain. The harbor of Dutch Harbor is protected to some degree by a long sand spit at the entrance. Dutch Harbor is on the Aleutian chain, a long way from Kodiak.

On our arrival, we were assigned quarters at Fort Mears, on flat land a short distance from the dock area. These wooden barracks had been occupied by army personnel prior to the Japanese bombing of Dutch Harbor. After the Japanese air raid, the army moved its personnel across the channel to Unalaska, where they were quartered in tents and temporary buildings. The army considered Fort Mears to be too much of a target for its combat personnel, since it anticipated another bombing. The army command at this base must have felt that Seabees were more expendable.

After getting our personnel settled at Fort Mears, we went about the job of planning our original overseas construction assignments. The civilian contractor here had lost many of his civilian personnel. They had returned to Seattle by the first available transportation—sea or air. There was a short airstrip at Dutch Harbor for PBYs [Consolidated PBY Catalina flying boat] and other small planes that could reach the mainland at Kodiak, for transfer to larger planes flying back to mainland USA. Despite the contractor's loss of personnel, his superintendent was hanging on tenaciously to the original contract with the navy to enlarge the base here. He was quite reluctant to release any part of the work to the 4th Seabees. Most of our early assignments were part of a housekeeping or maintenance nature, which did not require use of heavy equipment under control by the civilian contractor. On occasions we were permitted to use heavy equipment during off hours. A large part of the work here was of a waterfront nature, repairing and enlarging piers or wharves. Due to our dependence on the contractor for any equipment, we were usually limited to repairs to the barracks damaged by the Japanese bombing attack. It was obvious the civilian superintendent was doing everything to make life miserable for us and cause our mission to fail.

He was obviously reluctant to share any part of this lucrative contract with our Seabees. Since he controlled the construction equipment and materials, we were entirely at his mercy. This attitude was so obvious that one day I went to our skipper, Joe Bronson, and suggested that it was high time that we quit giving and start taking from the contractor. Joe was a patient fellow and told me we would just have to sweat it out for a little longer. He was right. After a few weeks, the superintendent had lost so many of his personnel that he began to ask us for our help. Now we had finally arrived and could begin to call the shots.

The 4th Seabees went through some rough times during our early days in Dutch Harbor. We finally got our chance to prove that we were a first-class construction outfit. We received praise from the army general who compared us favorably to the Army Corps of Engineers. The contractor's superintendent also gave us compliments for our waterfront construction and repairs to the barracks. Just when we felt we had been recognized as a first-class construction outfit, another cloud appeared on the horizon. Two navy CEC captains arrived without warning to make an inspection of our battalion. During their onsite inspection, they pointed out all the things that were wrong with our administration policies and lack of military posture. After completing their inspection, they advised that they would sojourn to Kodiak to make their unfavorable report to RADM John R. Reeves, the U.S. Navy line officer in charge of all navy operations in the Aleutians. They insisted that our skipper, Lieutenant Commander Bronson, accompany them to witness their charges of incompetence and lack of leadership within the battalion organization.

Our skipper flew out on a PBY[9] from Dutch Harbor to Kodiak with the two CEC captains from the Seattle office. At Kodiak they planned to advise Admiral Reeves regarding the "miserable" condition they found our battalion in at Dutch Harbor. Admiral Reeves was called "Jakey," but was known as "Blackjack." The navy captains told him the 4th Battalion was in such a mess that nothing short of one of them being placed in charge would suffice to straighten things out. "Blackjack" had received previous reports to the contrary from Brigadier General Holloway in Dutch Harbor and was prepared to deal with these would-be interlopers. He was also shrewd enough to understand their ploy. After listening courteously to their unfavorable report, he exploded furiously: "Get your asses out of here and go back to Seattle. This is the first time either of you have shown any interest in our Seabees, except to do your best to see that they failed on this, their original mission. Don't you ever come back to Dutch Harbor again without my permission." He then turned to Lieutenant Commander Bronson and told him to return to Dutch Harbor and report to General Holloway and take over navy construction from the civilian contractor. He said he would personally see to it that no other late-comers would be able to cut themselves in now that the Seabees had proven their worth at Dutch Harbor. He also said he planned to get in touch with Admiral Ben Moreell, our chief in Washington, D.C., and advise him of what he had just done to the two upstart captains, who had previously done all in their power to undermine the Seabees' program which Admiral Moreell had initiated. Finally, he said he would tell him he considered the 4th Seabees a rousing success in military construction.

Needless to say, we had no further interference from the "brass" in Seattle, and we were now able to pursue with all diligence the work at hand under the direction of the army command. We knew we had a loyal supporter and friend in "Blackjack" Reeves, who would keep the wolves from howling since we were the first battalion to go out on a mission as a unit. This was also a personal victory for our chief, Ben Moreell, who had originally conceived the idea of using construction battalions in the war

9. The PBY *Catalina* was a U.S. Navy flying boat that was used mainly for patrolling, although it could also be armed and used as an anti-submarine aircraft. *See* Simon Rigge and the Editors of Time-Life Books. *War in the Outposts*. (Alexandria, VA: Time-Life Books (World War II series), 1980, 28–29.

zone. The "old guard" officers preferred the old method of doing all navy work by civilian contractors and refused to recognize the wartime picture, where civilians could not work with any expectation of safety.

## Unalaska Island, Alaska

Late in July 1942, Co. A of the 4th Battalion was ordered to move across the channel from Dutch Harbor to the island of Unalaska. Co. "D" under Lt. (j.g) Clark Stroud went over with us. I was placed in charge of these two construction companies. Stroud became my executive officer. The junior medical officer of the battalion was assigned to us with a couple of hospital corpsmen. The medical officer, Stroud and I were quartered in a cabana, a small wooden, one-room building at our campsite. Our junior officers were quartered in other cabanas nearby. The petty officers and enlisted men were quartered in an uncompleted barracks building, which we proceeded to complete in short order. Included in the group from Co. D was my old highway buddy, Chief Pipkin, who was immediately placed in charge of all road building operations. He was quartered with the other chief petty officers in a section of the barracks building. We completed another barracks-type building and set up messing facilities.

After the [Japanese] bombing the army had dispersed their troops over to Unalaska. Their officers were quartered in cabanas built earlier by the native Aleuts. The men were quartered in tents. Our assignment was to build housing facilities, mess halls and roads for this army regiment. Since we were separated from the main body of our own battalion by a channel which used a ferry for crossing, we enjoyed the privilege of really being on our own. A young army captain acted as "liaison." We proceeded without delay to build roads, paths, Quonset hut quarters and mess halls for the army personnel.

Our detachment stationed here had two black stewards and 100 white enlisted men quartered in one of the barracks buildings. The chief petty officer in charge of completing this building set aside a separate room as quarters for the two stewards. The rest of the enlisted personnel were all in the large area of the barracks together. One of the stewards came to see Lieutenant (j.g.) Stroud, my executive officer, who was in charge of personal matters. My office was next door to Stroud's, so I could hear the conversation regarding the complaint the steward was making. "Mr. Stroud," the steward said, "you know we have two stewards cooped up in a tiny room separated from the other enlisted personnel." "Yes, I know," replied Stroud. "You should be happy to have private quarters like our chief petty officers, while the other men are crowded together in one large area." "But Mr. Stroud," the steward replied, "this ain't no Jim Crow Navy [*i.e.*, segregated]." "You are right," replied Stroud, "this is not a Jim Crow Navy, but there are a few old boys from Mississippi, Alabama, Georgia and Texas in the barracks that we do not know yet. So if I were those two fellows [*i.e.*, the stewards], I would just settle down in your private quarters and enjoy them." "Yes, Sir, Mr. Stroud," the steward replied and departed. We heard no more about this matter, and no incident ever occurred in the barracks. Needless to say, I was pleased by the way my fellow Texan, Lieutenant (j.g.) Stroud, had handled this "ticklish" situation. The stewards continued to serve the officer and chief petty officer messes in a professional manner.

Road construction in this army camp area was quite a challenge. Army personnel had tried to build a few key roads in their camp by conventional methods. They had scraped the vegetation from the tundra and then proceeded to get their tractors mired in the muskeg mud.[10] They had to spend a lot of time getting the stuck tractors from the muskeg mud, so they had made little progress. We placed CPO Pipkin, my old Texas highway associate, in full charge of all road work in the area. Even our young ensigns did not resent this unmilitary assignment [*i.e.*, having a CPO in command], since they knew by now that Pip knew his business. In lieu of removing the vegetation and exposing the muskeg mud, he arranged to place a thick layer of crushed rock from our quarry directly in the undisturbed area. True, this was an expensive design, but it proved effective. In a short period we were able to complete key roads and paths in the army camp area. This expedited delivery of building materials for completion of quarters and mess halls for the army. With some help from army personnel, we

10. "Muskeg" is a type of bog, "a thick, tensile blanket of vegetation." Simon Rigge and the Editors of Time-Life Books, *War in the Outposts* (Alexandria, VA: Time-Life Books, World War II series, 1980), 144–145.

were able to complete essential facilities before the autumn snows, rains and "williwaws" (Aleutian winds) set in.

Later on, a U.S. Army Corps of Engineers regiment under a full colonel came over to give us a hand toward completing our assignment. Initially, it was embarrassing to have this army colonel report to me, a navy lieutenant, for his job assignments each morning.[11] He did not seem to mind, since we were both professional engineers with comparable experience. Besides, General Holloway had told the colonel I was in charge of the project on Unalaska. With the help of the engineer regiment, we were able to complete our basic mission before foul weather came.

Lt. (j.g.) Ordis Forbess, another Texan and civil engineer graduate from Texas Tech in Lubbock, was in command of Co. B of the 4th Seabees. His company was stationed at the navy submarine base on the Dutch Harbor side. He too enjoyed a degree of autonomy for our battalion. His unit performed construction and maintenance work at this vital submarine base. Once I visited Lieutenant Forbess and had dinner with him and a young lieutenant who was the C.O. of a sub. He told me that once his submarine cleared the bar at Dutch Harbor, they had no friends. Even our own planes would drop depth charges on them. We had a nice dinner together and I wished him luck on their foray next day toward Kiska (in Japanese hands since June 1942). They never returned. The casualty rate on these small conventional subs was inordinately high. No wonder they drew "hazard" pay. I felt sad to think this nice young officer and his crew went down in the cold Aleutian waters. I was learning, first hand, what war was all about: it is cruel.

While my detachment was busy working for the army on Unalaska, our Company C was working for the navy, primarily on the waterfront jobs on Dutch Harbor Island. In order to expedite this vital waterfront work, they were reinforced by the arrival of another battalion, the 8th Seabees. The skipper of the 8th Battalion was a weird but brilliant lieutenant commander named Heflin, who had taught at Cal Tech before joining the navy Seabees. His executive officer, Lieut. "Hardrock" McKay, was a very competent officer who ran the battalion, while his skipper wandered in

11. A colonel is the equivalent of a navy captain, so he outranked my grandfather by four grades.

the hills of Unalaska with his carbine looking for any "yellow bellies" (Japanese) as he called them. Obviously, he never found any, since there were none on the island.[12]

Lt. Cmdr. Earl Kelly, a very competent officer out of the University of Colorado, had been detached from the 8th Battalion at Port Hueneme for duty in the Pacific. Then he showed up in Dutch Harbor. The navy sometimes does strange things. This created a problem for our skipper, Joe Bronson, who was now in charge of all construction in this sector. The problem was shortly resolved when our senior medical officer pronounced the "weird" lieutenant commander mentally incompetent to be stationed in a war zone. He received orders to return to Seattle by the first available transportation, which turned out to be a navy transport. On the day of his departure for Seattle, our junior medical officer, who was in the cabana with Stroud and me, was at the dockside when the navy transport sailed out. That evening he reiterated an amusing incident related to this event. He said Lieutenant McKay and other officers from the 8th Battalion were on the pier as the transport left the dock. They were with their backs to the snow covered Mount Ballyhoo behind them and the cold wind in their faces. The departing lieutenant commander leaned over the ship's rail and blurted out, "Who's crazy?" Probably not true—but still a good story about Lieutenant Commander Heflin's departure to the more balmy weather of Seattle.

On Unalaska, just across the channel from Dutch Harbor, there was an old small wood frame hotel that had gained a measure of fame. Jack London had lived there while writing his Alaskan stories and poems [during the Klondike Gold Rush in 1898]. In addition to the main building there were several cabanas, which served in earlier days as guest cottages for the hotel. Then, one fine day, we received word that another Seabee battalion was on its way to Dutch Harbor. This would be the 21st. My detachment was given the assignment to prepare quarters for this new battalion on Unalaska, using the old hotel and adjacent cabana. The earlier occupants were civilian workers with the construction company. Since most of them had departed and returned to the mainland, we were able to utilize this area for the incoming 21st. My troops

12. Unfortunately, racial slurs against the Japanese ran high in the Pacific War.

worked furiously to get this facility ready for the new battalion expected any day. It developed that they inherited better living quarters than my unit.

One of the officers was Lt. (j.g.) Clyde Trudell. He was a graduate architect from the University of California at Berkeley, as was my earlier friend Lt. Ray Peppin, whom I first met at Camp Allen on reporting for active duty. Clyde and I became fast friends. After he finished college, he had a very interesting job. He worked on the plans for Rockefeller on the restoration of Williamsburg to its original colonial appearance. Later, he authored a book on Colonial Yorktown, which was published.[13] We continued our friendship after the war. For a period of time, he served as an officer in my Seabee Reserve Battalion at Treasure Island. Clyde died on November 12, 1978, and we attended his military funeral at Mt. Tamalpais Cemetery in San Rafael. With additional help from the 21$^{st}$, we were able to complete construction of the basic facilities for the army on Unalaska and work with our own camp and maintenance of army roads.

Just as I was able to settle down from the rat-race and take life a little easier, another surprise job came my way. Skipper Joe Bronson was called to Washington to complete plans for the formation of the last Seabee regiment. We now had three battalions in the area which qualified us for regimental status. Neil Kingsley, Joe's executive officer, then went to Washington to relieve Joe to complete plans for the new regiment. So, I was ordered back to Dutch Harbor to be executive officer to Lieutenant Commander— now Commander—Bronson, while Neil was away. Doing administrative work was a new experience. I preferred my job in Unalaska. However I caught on to my duties there in short order.

## Dutch Harbor

I worked hard in my job as acting executive officer in the 4$^{th}$ Seabee Battalion. I spent long hours at the office doing administrative work—for which I had little navy training. There were never any

---

13. Clyde Trudell, *Colonial Yorktown: Being a Brief Historie of the Place; Together with Something of its Houses and Publick Buildings* (Richmond, VA: The Dietz Press, 1938). The author gave my father an autographed copy, which we still have in our home library.

dull moments keeping up with the pace set by "Jumping Joe" Bronson, our skipper. Shortly after I took over as executive, I found out that there were a few warrant officer billets open for superior chief petty officers. Somewhat against his will, I was able to persuade my old friend CPO Pipkin to apply for warrant officer status. He was still building roads in Unalaska under Lieutenant (j.g.) Stroud and was quite satisfied in his present position. He finally agreed to apply, with some reluctance, so we forwarded his application, with a strong endorsement, to Washington, and brought back news that our Civil Engineer Corps was short of lieutenants to fill billets in new battalions now being formed. With Neil's help, I was able to persuade "Pip" to submit an application for a commission as a lieutenant in the CEC. "Pip" thought we were crazy, since he had just submitted his application for warrant officer rank. However, Neil Kingsley, who knew "all the ropes" in matters such as this, sent dispatches back to the Navy Department in Washington in support of this latest application.

To my surprise and delight, we received information that "Pip" had been approved as a full lieutenant. Now, we looked forward to adding "Pip" to our officer staff in the 4th Seabees. However, to our dismay, he received orders to report back to Seattle for indoctrination prior to being ordered to duty with a new battalion. When "Pip" arrived in Seattle, his commission as a warrant officer was on hand, and they wanted to swear him in as a warrant officer. He got in touch with us at Dutch Harbor and we told him to sit tight and wait for the lieutenant's commission, which was on its way.

Shortly thereafter he was sworn in as a full lieutenant, Civil Engineer Corps, U.S. Navy, and proceeded with indoctrination prior to being ordered to one of the newly formed battalions. Needless to say, I was proud to have been a party to his deserved promotion. I had known him since 1930, where we first met at the Highway Department in Waco, Texas. I had always considered him to be a smarter civil engineer than I. After the war, he continued in the reserve program and retired in Fort Worth as a full commander. Our friendship has continued until this day [before he passed away].

Lieutenant Commander Bronson proceeded rapidly with plans to establish the last Seabee regiment at Dutch Harbor, with himself as officer-in-charge, and a spot promotion to the rank of commander.

Neil would then become OINC of the 4th Seabee Battalion with a "spot" to lieutenant commander.[14] Then, I would become executive officer of the battalion. Just as we were preparing for the above changes, we received word that a small Seabee detachment, under one of our CEC Ensigns at Atka Island, further west on the chain, was getting pushed around by an army colonel on the island. The problem involved site selection for "Navy Town" on Atka. A decision was made to send me out there on "Temporary Duty Orders" to try to straighten out the problem with the army command. So, on October 29, 1942, I received orders to report to the captain of the USS *Teal*, a seaplane tender, for transportation to Atka on temporary duty orders.

## Aboard the USS Teal

My transportation from Dutch Harbor to Atka Island was provided for by this small seaplane tender. The trip was something less than a pleasure cruise. En route we had winds up to 60 knots, which buffeted this small ship unmercifully. No one dared go on deck for fear of being washed overboard. All we had to eat was sandwiches and coffee, which we each prepared from the pantry. The galley was closed due to the storm. The mess room was never crowded. I managed to avoid getting seasick but was alarmed when we started getting submarine "contacts" on the ship's screen. I remembered that a sister ship to the *Teal* had been hit just as they were entering Nazen Bay, the so-called harbor of Atka Island, several weeks before. The skipper of that vessel beached the tender and no lives were lost. Our Seabees at Atka welded a temporary patch on the hull where the torpedo entered and she was able to limp back to Dutch Harbor for further repairs, and later to Seattle for dry dock. After two miserable days, we arrived at Atka without being hit.

## Atka Island, Alaska

I disembarked from the *Teal* in Nazen Bay by small boat and was met at the beach by our ensign, who drove me in his jeep to his quarters. Having been refreshed with food and a nap, after my perilous voyage from Dutch Harbor, the ensign briefed me on his

14. A "spot promotion" is a promotion to the next higher rank where the job requires higher rank.

problem with the army command. His request for a "Navy Town" site on high ground overlooking the harbor had been denied. Also, the colonel had not cooperated in the loan of some essential equipment, such as trucks and a tractor. These were needed if the ensign could proceed with his mission. My job was to straighten this all out. It was obvious that our ensign and his small band of Seabees were being put off or ignored by this army colonel. He had told the ensign that he was too busy with higher priorities to concern himself with their problems, which he considered minor. The ensign was completely "at sea," since he found it difficult to communicate with the colonel due to the great difference in rank. Obviously, my work was cut out for me!

The next day after my arrival on Atka Island, I went to call on the colonel in charge of the army regiment on the island. I hoped to be able to work out the problem of securing cooperation with the small navy detachment so they could fulfill their mission on the island. The colonel was not in his office but was out on an army power barge anchored in Nazen Bay. This barge was used to transport supplies, materials and equipment ashore from cargo ships anchored in the bay. The occasion of the colonel's visit to the power barge was the rather sudden death of the barge captain due to a heart attack the day before. The colonel went out to arrange bringing the body ashore for burial. The corpse had been placed in a plain pine box, built on the barge, from "dunnage" (scrap lumber) from the hold of the cargo ship. I went down to the dock to meet the colonel and the men bringing the body ashore. On arrival I met the colonel. We followed the men carrying the pine box with the body to a small cabana up a hill. This cabana was for the one-teacher school here. The door to the cabana was too narrow to take the box through, so I assisted in lifting the body by hand it and carrying it to a kitchen table inside. I joined the colonel here in shaving and bathing the departed captain and dressing him in clean clothes for the burial. I even tied a tie to the body. We then lifted the body through the narrow door and placed it back in the pine box out on the porch. I attended the simple funeral in the nearby village cemetery. The colonel gave the captain full military honors, although he was a civilian. I was visibly impressed with the colonel's concern in bringing the captain ashore for burial rather than burial at sea in the bay.

This concern on the part of the colonel for the deceased made me feel that we could do business. This unusual introduction paved the way for friendly communication. He knew, of course, that I was the personnel representative of Admiral Reeves in Kodiak, where his boss, a major general, also resided. After the funeral, we repaired to the colonel's office, where I explained my mission and presented a request for title to the desired real estate for Navy Town. He granted this request forthwith, as we both smiled at the prospect that anyone would quarrel over any wasteland on this desolate island. The colonel also agreed to furnish the navy detachment with construction equipment and to deliver supplies and building materials to expedite the construction of Navy Town. My mission was done so easily and quickly that the young navy ensign marveled at my diplomatic coup. I explained that our cause was helped by the barge captain's death, giving the colonel and me time to get acquainted as "amateur morticians." I was happy to have accomplished this "temporary duty" in a single day. Now I would be able to return to Dutch Harbor and resume my duties as executive officer of the 4th Seabees. However, I faced the problem of hitching a ride back to Dutch Harbor. The USS *Teal* had already sailed west and there was no obvious way for sea or air transportation from Atka to Dutch Harbor. I figured that if I could find a ride to Adak Island, further west on the chain, I could catch a navy PBY (called "Yokeboats") back to Dutch.

After a few days wondering how I would be able to return to Dutch Harbor from Atka, I was informed that I could hitch a ride to Adak on a PBY which the navy had loaned to the Army Air Corps. This amphibious plane had just landed in Nazen Bay and was operated by two young army second lieutenants. They had just secured the plane from the navy and were on practice runs. Since this plane could land on both land and water, the army intended to use it in rescue operations. If I had known this was the first experience of this pilot and co-pilot, I might have been reluctant to take a chance with them. However, this seemed the best chance I had to get to Adak and then back to Dutch Harbor, so I ferried out by small boat and boarded the PBY. I was the only passenger.

## Adak, Alaska

It was early in November 1942 when I arrived in Adak. This was the last large island in the Aleutian chain west of Dutch Harbor that was still in our hands. Kiska and Attu had been taken over and occupied by the Japanese in June 1942 (and held until mid-1943). The Japanese occupation in the Aleutians and concern that they could attack the West Coast from there was when the U.S. began Operation SANDCRAB. At once I sensed the feverish activity on this island to establish an outpost against the enemy to the west. This was truly in the war zone. The harbor, called "Sweeper's Cove," is a sheltered bay for our warships, seaplanes and cargo ships. A high mountain overlooks the flat area developed into a military base.

On my arrival at Adak I "logged in" with Lt. Sam Hamill at the navy communications station. I explained that I needed to return to Dutch Harbor on the first available transportation. He smiled and said: "I don't think you will be returning to Dutch for a while. We have a dispatch for you from Lt. Commander Bronson at Dutch." This dispatch stated that I was to take charge of a 50-man 4th Seabee Detachment under Ensign Anderson with a mission to build "Navy Town" on Adak. A Lieutenant Fuller had been in charge of this detachment, which had been engaged in assembling pontoon barges on the beach at Sweepers Cove. These barges were formed by placing hollow steel boxes in the stern with a heavy duty outboard engine. Others were simple flat barges used in unloading materials, equipment and personnel from ship to shore in Sweeper's Cove. There were no docks for ships to tie up at Sweeper's Cove.

Lieutenant Fuller had recently boarded a ship to return to Dutch Harbor to arrange for supplies and more pontoon parts. This freighter caught on fire in the harbor the night before sailing. Several people died and Lieutenant Fuller was badly burned. He had been evacuated by plane to the navy hospital in Kodiak for treatment a few days before my arrival in Adak. The dispatch orders gave me a relief for Lieutenant Fuller; however I was given a new mission. I inherited a young redheaded ensign from Texas, 50 Seabees, and one jeep, with a mission to build "Navy Town" which involved quarters and messing facilities for naval aviators being ordered to Adak. It was assumed that I would get logistical support from an army engineer regiment already on the island. Incidentally, I had known my redheaded ensign's brother back in the Texas State Highway Department before the war. My mission on the island presented quite a challenge with no equipment— except the lone jeep.

Our mission on Adak was urgent. Naval personnel, especially naval aviators, were arriving daily on the island and were being quartered in tents. We were already in November and the stormy Aleutian winter was near at hand. We needed to get them out of tents as soon as possible and into Quonsets for housing and messing. My 50-man Seabee detachment had no trucks or other equipment, except the lone jeep, so we must depend on the army for help. An army engineer regiment, under a West Point lieutenant colonel, were working feverishly on a fighter airstrip in the adjacent valley. This facility was sorely needed to protect us from enemy air raids. The army graciously delivered our supplies and construction materials (lumber and Quonset hut parts) from the waterfront to our storage area in Navy Town. We were able to borrow a D-4 tractor and "Athey" trailer (equipped with moving treads, rather than wheels) from the army to haul construction materials from the storage area to construction sites over the sticky tundra. Any other equipment would be mired in the soft tundra mud.

With this aid from the army, we made rapid progress with Navy Town construction. However, one fine morning, the army engineers came and reclaimed the D-4 Tractor and "Athey" trailer. This practically shut us down. The West Point lieutenant colonel told this lowly navy lieutenant that he hated to do this to us, but the airstrip had "top priority" and needed every available piece of equipment to meet their deadline. In desperation, I took off in our jeep to see General Landrum, the island commander, to request return of the tractor and trailer. When I arrived at his tent office, I noted that this gentleman (from Florida) was sitting outside his tent, smoking a pipe and "whittling" on a piece of wood with his pocket knife. Then I knew I was in for trouble, since it is common knowledge that a man who whittles while smoking a pipe is usually very deliberate. The general expressed his concern for my problem, but supported the army engineer's claim to reclaim the equipment due to the top priority of the airstrip. He also said he failed to understand why the great U.S. Navy could not furnish ample equipment for their newest toy—the Seabees—rather than depend on the army for logistic support. He dismissed me by stating he agreed with the lieutenant colonel of the army engineers that the airstrip was more important than our navy facilities.

I returned to my office, rather disconsolate at this turn of events. Lieutenant Hamill from navy communications was waiting for me with a dispatch from Admiral Reeves in Kodiak. The gist of the message was that since Adak had no guns for coastal defense against any element of the Japanese fleet [Imperial Japanese Navy, or IJN], he was sending a 6" naval gun to the island commander, and my Seabee detachment should assist in setting up this battery. This message gave me an idea to approach the general for return of the equipment. I drove back out to see General Landrum and said: "Sir, I am prepared to offer you a "6" naval gun for coastal defense and my Seabees will help with the installation on the site you may choose." He replied: "Are you sure you can do this—and just what is it going to cost me?" I replied in the affirmative and stated that the cost would be the trailer and tractor that was taken from us this morning. I was surprised to have won so quickly and easily. I left the general with his promise that the engineers would return the equipment to us forthwith, which they did. We were able to feverishly continue our mission to build Navy Town.

Since I had known that navy communications were faster than those of the army, I was able to deal with the general with my first hand-information about the gun. A little later, the general found out about the dispatch from Admiral Reeves and sent for me. He asked: "Ritter, why didn't you tell me about the dispatch from Kodiak." I said: "General, you did not ask me why I was able to promise you the 6" gun." He then said: "You win—a deal is a deal— you can keep the equipment, but I will still be waiting for you the next time around." Fortunately, we managed to finish before the "next time around."

Shortly thereafter, the 6" naval gun arrived by ship and was hauled up a high point overlooking the entrance to Sweeper's Cove. My Seabees assisted in pouring the base for the gun and helping to complete its installation. Now we felt more secure against attacks on the island from Japanese naval vessels.

Just as we had completed barracks and messing facilities for naval aviators and ourselves, I received authorization to construct a navy pier. The location of the pier was in Sweeper's Cove adjacent to Navy Town. On first blush, this appeared to be a Herculean task for our little 50-man Seabee detachment. However, I remembered the army had a huge barge with a pile driver attached. I enlisted the support of the army engineers to drive the piling, who then let us place the superstructure. Piling and bridge timbers for the structure arrived shortly by cargo ship. These materials for the pier were unloaded by the army and transported to the pier site. The army engineers were happy to use their pile driving equipment, since this did not interfere with their work on the air strip for the island. Also, they would be able to use our navy dock to unload cargo ships, rather than off-loading on barges and then to trucks. The sea was often quite rough in the cove. After the engineers drove the piling, our Seabees placed the timber caps and superstructure in short order. We hurried to finish the pier in anticipation of winter weather, which would have seriously hampered unloading the cargo ships. Now our supplies and materials would no longer be dependent on the army for this logistic support.

On completion of Navy Town and the pier, a squadron of naval air was transferred to Adak. Their aircraft were primarily PBY's (called "Yokeboats"). They were amphibians, since they could take off and land on sea or land. They were well suited to conditions in the Aleutians with the fog, rain, snow, and unpredictable weather. Although this plane was designed primarily for rescue missions, they were given other duties here in Adak. They were also used to transport troops and supplies. They were also used to accompany Army Air Force B-24s on bombing missions over Kiska Island, one of the Aleutian Islands now in Japanese hands. Our PBY's went along on the Kiska raids primarily to navigate for the army bombers, since the navy excelled in this area; however, they often actively participated in dropping bombs on enemy positions. These planes were slow and clumsy and were prime targets for Japanese anti-aircraft gunners protecting their base in Kiska.

Quite a few of our ensign pilots and their crews failed to return from these missions. There was a squadron of P-40 fighter planes on Adak now, but Kiska was out of their cruising range. The army engineers had substantially completed the air strip at Adak and it was in full operation. Two very special officers flew out that day on the Kiska run. When they failed to return that night, I grieved at the apparent loss of these two fine young men and their crews. Then to our surprise and delight, they returned to Adak the next morning. They told us that on their return they encountered a very thick fog and selected a quiet bay to set the planes down and spend the night. They floated all night on this bay, and then took off early the next morning for the return to their base at Adak. The navy had some very versatile personnel, including our own Seabees.

Early in December 1942 (a year after Pearl Harbor), I received orders from Kodiak to build a seaplane facility on Andrew Lagoon, which was over the mountain and on the other side of the island from Navy Town. This so-called lagoon was actually a lake, about 10-feet above normal sea level. There were no safe enclosures as an anchorage for boats or barges from sea to transport Quonset materials needed to construct facilities for this seaplane base. There were, of course, no roads over the mountain for overland transport. Also, it would be virtually impossible to take supplies and materials in by sea due to the constant rough weather and no suitable landing area on the shore line at the mouth of the lagoon (lake). Leave it to the navy to dream up a seemingly impossible task for the Seabees. Our line command in Kodiak must have been sold on our "Can Do" motto and another saying: "Difficult jobs done right away— impossible ones take a little longer."

After a few sleepless nights pondering on how to solve this dilemma, I devised a plan to get personnel, supplies and Quonset parts to the site needed to build this facility. I persuaded the PBY Squadron commander to allow his pilots returning from a mission to fly over the mountain, land on the lagoon and taxi up to shore with men, supplies and building materials (Quonsets). The plan to use PBY's to transport men and materials across the mountain to Andrew Lagoon to accomplish our mission of building a sea plane base worked like a charm. The PBY pilots seemed to enjoy this diversion and became quite expert in landing and take-offs from the lagoon, as well as taxiing up to the shoreline to permit discharge of their load. With this primary assistance, and some help from the assigned staff for this base, we were able to complete the project in short order. This was a very interesting exercise in logistics. I attended the commissioning ceremony at this seaplane base, and noted the squadron of navy seaplanes anchored in the lagoon, ready to intercept any air or sea attack on Adak. My Seabees were highly praised at the ceremony for accomplishing this difficult mission.

A short time after the seaplane base was placed in operation, Admiral "Blackjack" Reeves flew in from Kodiak to inspect this new facility on Adak. He stopped by Dutch Harbor in his personal PBY to pick up Captain McKenna, a line captain who was directly responsible for the operation of this seaplane base. When they arrived in Adak, he sent for me and insisted that I accompany them for the inspection tour of the seaplane base. I suggested that we fly over in one of our PBY's stationed in Adak, since the local pilots were familiar, by experience, with this operation. The admiral overruled me and insisted that his personal pilot "Bull" Dawson take us over to Andrew Lagoon in the admiral's personal PBY. The admiral was a naval aviator and acted as co-pilot. He insisted that I act as navigator, since I had made this trip many times during the construction of the facility. I managed to get us down on the lagoon at the proper spot, but when our pilot tried to taxi up to the shore line— as the local pilots had done many times—the plane began to spin its wheels in the loose sand and gravel bottom of the shallow water. I was afraid we would bog down and then would have to be towed back to deeper water. The admiral must have shared my fears, for he turned to me asked: "What shall we do now?" I suggested that we have his pilot turn around and get back to deeper water before we became mired. Now, I was sure that he agreed with my earlier suggestion that we use a local pilot familiar with this operation of taxiing out to the shoreline. When we reached the deeper water allowing the PBY to float, we dropped anchor and signaled for a small boat to come out and pick up our party. All this had taken considerably more time, delaying our inspection of the facility. A red-headed 1st class petty officer came out from the base in a small motor boat and took us ashore.

The petty officer seemed to be in charge of the camp; however, as we toured the area, no one seemed to be in charge. Everything about the place was dirty and untidy, including the galley. The facility had a rundown appearance, reflecting poor maintenance. Even the bunks in the quarters' area were unmade. Two soldiers were asleep in the barracks and did not even get up to salute the flag officer. I was walking right behind the admiral and noted the veins sticking out on his neck, so I was sure he was about to blow his stack. Suddenly, he turned around and bellowed his displeasure at me. It was quite a tirade, for which I did not blame him, except for his singling me out for his lecture. Of course, I had no responsibility for the camp's operation and not been here since the commissioning. I turned toward Captain McKenna, who was the responsible officer, expecting him to tell the admiral the lecture should have directed to him, rather than me. To my dismay, the captain remained silent. Then the admiral yelled: "Let's get out of this crummy place!" We returned to our plane for the trip back to the main base at Adak.

When we left the plane at the strip in Adak, the admiral dismissed Captain McKenna and asked me to accompany him for an inspection of the navy pier we had built in Sweeper's Cove. I followed him at a respectful distance, still smarting from the lashing I had received at the Seabee base. He motioned me to come alongside and said: "Ritter, I know you are not responsible for the condition of the camp we just inspected." He gave me a gracious smile and continued: "But you were just standing too damn close to me at the time. You and your Seabees did an excellent job under insurmountable conditions, and I am very proud of the job you did. Captain McKenna should have risen to your rescue. I will suggest that he give you a letter of commendation for a job well done."

After our return from the inspection of the sea plane facility on Andrew Lagoon, we accompanied Admiral Reeves to the navy pier that the 4th Seabee Detachment had built with logistical support from the army engineers. He was duly impressed at the quality workmanship performed here with our 50-man detachment. He said our performance in building Navy Town, the new navy pier, and the seaplane facility was remarkable and highly commendable. Now I knew for sure that the Seabees had a real supporter in this line rear admiral.

A few days after the admiral's departure, I received a dispatch from Cmdr. Joe Bronson to come to Dutch Harbor on another mission further west. Apparently "Jumping Joe" felt that with my farm background I qualified as a "Pioneer." I had hoped to return to the main body of the 4th Battalion after completing my tasks at Adak. Now, it seemed that Joe had other plans for me. My first available transportation back to Dutch Harbor came suddenly and without advance warning. A B-24 Bomber was leaving in one bound for Dutch Harbor, so I had to hustle to get down to the plane on the strip at Adak. Our plane had no sooner left Adak when a blinding fog closed in on the strip. There was no way the B-24 could return and land—which is what the pilots wanted to do with this sudden change in weather conditions over the Aleutians between Adak and Dutch. Due to the miserable fog and wind and the relatively short runway, our pilot decided to try an emergency landing at Umnak Island. I was standing behind the co-pilot and could not see anything through the thick fog below. I could not possibly see how the pilot could sit us down here. As we descended, at almost the level of the airstrip there, our pilot caught a glimpse of a piece of runway through the dense fog. He made a sharp dive for the runway and touched down about half way down this short runway. We all hung on as he braked the plane and turned off at the last taxi-way. Our plane almost rolled over as we made this right angle turn on two wheels. As our plane took this severe port list, I could see the Bering Sea staring at us just over the cliff. How our pilot ever got away with that landing and turning onto the last taxi-way I will never know. Finally, we came to a stop, much to our relief. This had really been a close call, demonstrating the training and skill of our pilot. It was good to be back on "Terra Firma."

We were grounded on Umnak Island for several days due to a blizzard. Our B-24 pilot elected to return to Adak as soon as the weather cleared. He was afraid of the short runway at Dutch Harbor with the constantly changing weather conditions at this time of year in the Aleutians. I was told that I could catch a ride to Dutch on a navy PBY in a few days. Adjacent to this airstrip, I noted a few small spruce trees enclosed by a high fence. Since there were no trees on this part of the Aleutian chain, these bushes fascinated this country boy from the piney woods of East Texas. I was told these bushes had been sent from Seattle as Christmas trees and the boys at this airfield had immediately replanted them. A big sign on the high fence enclosure read: "National Umnak Forest." Quite a sense of humor demonstrated by the personnel here at this lonely outpost.

A navy PBY arrived at Umnak and I boarded her for a ride to Dutch Harbor. When we arrived at Dutch, our PBY pilot touched down too far out on this short runway. We could not brake the plane down soon enough to stop at the end of the runway, so we went down a slope and stopped with the tail of our plane high in the air. The ground crew had to bring ladders to get us out of the plane. Fortunately, no one was injured in this overrun. This had been quite an exercise for me, getting from Adak back to Dutch, but now I was back home with the main body of my beloved 4th Battalion. It had been almost two months since I left here for temporary duty headed for Atka Island and then to Adak Island. So many things had happened to me since I left here, that it seemed much longer. Anyway, I was back home to ascertain what future mission was in store for me. I was allowed a short visit with my former comrades, including the detachment on adjacent Unalaska. It was good to visit my old buddies again.

## Dutch Harbor

After my short visit with my former associates in the 4th Seabees, I reported to Skipper Joe Bronson for word on my next assignment. He told me that the army planned to occupy an island west of Adak about half way to Kiska. Kiska, one of the islands in our Aleutian chain, was in enemy hands. It was not known whether the "Island X" we were going to was occupied by the Japanese. If so, there would be an assault to capture the Island. Colonel Mark Logie would take about 1000 men from the army at Dutch on this mission. It was proposed that I go along so there would be navy representation and especially Seabee participation in occupying an island close to the enemy. I was further encouraged to accept the assignment (as if I had a choice) by being given a spot promotion to lieutenant commander, so that I would have a little more rank to deal with high ranking army officers. Also, the job in Adak was becoming routine—mostly housekeeping and maintenance. The plan called for me to go ashore with Lieutenant Hamill, communications officer at Adak, and four petty officers from my detachment at Adak. Our mission was to ensure that the navy got a suitable site on the island for building Navy Town (shades of my earlier mission to Atka Island). Later, Ensign Jeffus would join us with 50-Seabees from Dutch to construct Navy Town on this Island. I would be under the direct command of Captain McKenna, the Navy Line Commander at Dutch Harbor. I would report to Colonel Logie, who would be my direct superior on Island "X." I met Colonel Logie at Dutch and instinctively liked him. He was tall with greying hair and looked the part of a real soldier and leader.

My participation in this mission was firmed up with Colonel Logie and I was given secret plans and orders. Now I began to look forward to the mission as a fulfillment of earlier training we had received back in Virginia [in the spring of 1942]. Since my mission to Dutch Harbor was over, I planned to return to Adak and await further orders. This time I boarded a dependable PBY and left Dutch Harbor in a torrential rain and landed in Adak in a dense fog. Normal weather for this time of year, December, in the Aleutians.

## Adak Island

On my return to Adak, I was given an unusual assignment. My detachment was ordered to build a Magazine Quonset in the hills, some distance from the air strip. This magazine would be used to transfer all the poison gas bombs from a location adjacent to the air field to a more secure location. This was the first time that I knew we had poison gas around. The primary reason for the transfer was to prevent accidental loading and subsequent dropping of gas bombs on the enemy at Kiska.[15] It was also necessary to protect ourselves from an accident in case of an enemy air raid that might set these poison gas bombs off nearer our air field. The job had to be done with utmost caution and secrecy, in order to avoid the anxiety of other military personnel on the island. We completed this mission in short order. I was very happy to have this behind us.

Just before Christmas 1942, "Skipper" Joe Bronson paid us a visit in Adak to inspect various projects our detachment had completed. Also, he said he would discuss my mission further with Colonel Logie. He had no sooner said that when he went down with the flu. He was too sick to attend our Christmas party at Navy Town. He spent a miserable day in bed during his first visit to Adak. Since he could not attend our Christmas party, I brought him a few gifts that were distributed at the mess hall. These gifts had been sent out by the Navy Wives Club in Seattle. Joe was just like a little kid getting toys for Christmas. He said he would always remember Christmas at Adak.

15. On December 20, 1942, the USAAF began bombing, strafing, and incendiary attacks on Japanese installations at Kiska Harbor. "Chronology of San Francisco War Events: 1942: Japanese Internment to Guadalcanal," http://www.sfmuseum. net/1906/ww2.html. See also Simon Rigge and the Editors of Time-Life Books, *War in the Outposts*, 130–132.

As soon as Joe recovered, he inspected the facilities we had built on the island. Then, we formed plans for my mission to Island "X," which we expected to begin in early January 1943. Before he left for Dutch Harbor, he made our little 4th Seabee Detachment proud with his sincere praise for our accomplishments under difficult circumstances. He returned to Dutch Harbor to his new command as Officer-in-Charge of the 1st. C.B. Regiment.

Shortly after Commander Bronson left Adak to return to Dutch Harbor, we were surprised by the arrival of 100 Seabees under the command of a CEC lieutenant commander. They had been sent directly to Adak from Seattle, bypassing the newly established 1st. Regiment at Dutch Harbor. On the arrival of 100 new Seabees under a full lieutenant commander, I was no longer the senior officer on Adak. My spot promotion to lieutenant commander had not yet come through officially. Even if it had, the new officer would out rank my "spot." It was obvious that those two ranking CEC Officers in DIPRACDOCKS in Seattle were at it again. They were still trying to "get into the act" by bypassing the 1st Regiment. This newly arrived lieutenant commander had been a professor at Cal Tech in Los Angeles with little or no practical experience. Anyway, he started out fast to throw his weight around. It was plain to see that he could easily destroy all the fine rapport we had been able to establish with the army—which had really paid off. He could also mess up our fine relations with other naval units on the island. I persuaded him not to make me his executive officer, but rather allow me to be his liaison with the army engineers. In this way, I was able to repair some of the early damage he had done to our relationship. With this sudden turn of events, I was more than anxious to "get the hell out of Adak" and accompany the army on my next mission to Island "X."

# Chapter 2

✦

✦

✦

✦

✦

# 1943: Still in the Aleutians

My desire to leave Adak was fulfilled in a short time. On January 9, 1943, I received orders from Captain McKenna at Dutch Harbor to report to Lieutenant Sam Hamill, our communications officer, on matters regarding our new mission. Sam advised us that our orders were to sail on the *North Coast*, a cargo ship, with four selected petty officers, on their arrival from Dutch on the *Middleton*, a Coast Guard ship. Ensign Jeffus would arrive on the *North Coast* with 50 Seabees and remain on Adak until we could prepare a place from them on Island "X." Ensign Jeffus arrived with the 50 Seabees on the *North Coast* as planned on January 12, 1943, and I received orders to depart on the *North Coast* with Lieutenant Hamill and the four petty officers for a rendezvous with the army units who had already departed. We sailed out of Adak, ostensibly, for Umnak Island; however our Island "X" location had been suddenly changed. We went east of Kiska, where the Japanese were entrenched. We dropped anchor in an unsheltered bay, right by the enemy's back door, and with winter storms approaching. We wondered if Amchitka was still occupied by the Japanese and whether an assault would be made by the army. While awaiting further orders, I had time to wonder what fate might have in store for us on the lonely looking Island "X."

## Amchitka Island, Alaska

The island of Amchitka is a high plateau with a valley on one side leading out to the Bering Sea. A short while after our cargo ship *North Coast* dropped anchor, our small party of two officers and four petty officers went ashore in an LCM (small landing craft). Like those who landed before us, we got up to our knees wading ashore from the LCM. That Aleutian water was really cold in January. We carried our gear ashore, including the tent which would be our initial home on this desolate island. When I climbed the bluff to the high ground, which would be the Navy Area, I saw Col. Mark Logie standing straight in the wind. He was bare-headed, since he had lost his cap during the landing. When I inquired how things were, he said the enemy had been on the island a short while ago, as noted by the signs; however, there was no evidence that any Japanese had remained. He pointed out toward Kiska and said: "They (the Japanese) are over there with 10,000 men—we have 1000 troops ashore—so we think we have them covered." Somehow, this gave me the assurance I needed on our arrival at our first Island "X." He noted however, that the [U.S.] Coast Guard transport *Middleton* had dropped anchor in a strong wind on their arrival and had run aground. The ship's bow was on the beach and she was really dead in the water. The colonel pointed out the place where we could set up our tent; however he advised digging foxholes as the first order of business. He expected the Japanese in Kiska would know we were there and would probably send seaplanes over with their calling cards (bombs) at any time.

On our arrival, we set up a tent on a bluff overlooking the open bay to the east. This site would later become Navy Town. This tent would serve as quarters for the two officers and four petty officers for the time being. We ate our K-rations in silence and then went outside where each person dug his own foxhole. These would be our stations in the event of an enemy air raid—which seemed very probable. By this time, we were tired, so we retired for the night and all had a good night's sleep.

Next morning, Lt. Sam Hamill (the other officer in our party) and I set out to explore our area to make a preliminary survey for establishing a navy facility. We were some distance from our foxholes adjacent to our tent quarters when we heard the clear sound of approaching aircraft. The angry nature of the sound made it clear to us that they were not ours. Obviously, they were enemy aircraft. Soon we sighted three seaplanes approaching from the west and flying toward us. This was a unique experience for each of us—our first encounter with our enemy, the Japanese. There was no time to return to our foxholes, so we dived into a nearby gulley and lay flat on our stomachs with our helmets on. I turned slightly as the planes passed directly over us and noted the Rising Sun insignia on the wings of the planes. No doubt about it, these were our visitors from Kiska. Suddenly we felt a dull thud and were spattered with tundra mud. One of the planes had dropped a bomb near us. We were frightened, but not injured. Sam rolled over toward me, and I noted that his helmet was covered with mud—the splash from the bomb dropped nearby. Then he exclaimed: "Rex, I think those SOB's are trying to kill us!" This broke the spell of our fears and I replied: "Sam, I think you are right; however, they failed this time." We turned and looked toward the bay. We noted a few bombs dropping in the water with a great splash; however, none of the anchored ships appeared to have been hit. Obviously, the Japanese bombers were poor marksmen. The bomb that landed about 100 feet from us left a gaping hole in the tundra. This first raid caused no casualties or apparent damage; however, we knew they would return. Our only protection was a few 20-mm guns on the ships in the bay and a few 37-mm antiaircraft guns ashore. Their seaplanes could easily fly above the range of these weapons.

After the raid, the army engineers started working furiously on a fighter strip in the valley so that we might get some of our fighter planes on the island to give us some protection from the Japanese air raids. In the late afternoon of the same day, more "Pontoon Joe's from Tokyo" paid us a second visit. They managed to stay out of range of our antiaircraft gun. There were no casualties or damage from this second attack. Maybe they just wanted us to know they were here, and perhaps might choose to leave, since we were so exposed. Our greatest danger was from the wild firing of our own antiaircraft guns—especially the army 37-mm battery, a short distance from our campsite. These guns literally "cut the grass" in our area, so that we had to stay low in our foxholes. All in all, these raids were just like we had seen in movies—only these were for real.[1]

The enemy seaplanes continued to call on us, morning and afternoon. You could set your watch by their daily arrivals. One afternoon a few days later, at the sound of the air raid warning, two army enlisted men jumped into their deep foxholes on a hillside adjacent to our camp. After the raid, several of us surveyed the scene to assess the damage from the bombs dropped on the slope near where the airstrip was under construction by the army engineers. We noted a bomb crater adjacent to the large foxhole which had been covered by the soil fallout. I started digging furiously into the foxhole with a shovel, which suddenly touched a body. We found that both of the soldiers had been buried alive in the foxhole. This was quite an experience to discover our first casualties—this would not be our last. Despite the daily visits of the Japanese seaplanes, we made progress with our initial mission to set up the advance base to receive our reinforcements.

Ensign Jeffus (another Texan) arrived with the 50-man Seabee detachment from the original 4th Battalion. "Doc" Bigger, the senior medical officer of the battalion, came along. Skipper Joe Bronson thought we could use a medical officer here—and besides, "Doc" wanted a change of scenery from Dutch Harbor and a chance to be in the war zone. "Doc" built a special foxhole with a built-in seat so he could watch the show during the air raids. A tracer from the 37-mm battery down the hill from our campsite buried into the wall of his foxhole, but fortunately just missed the good doctor, who was occupying the foxhole at the time. During this raid, the Japanese wiped out that 37-mm battery and killed three gunners— one of their first direct hits.

With the arrival of Ensign Jeffus and his 50 Seabees, we were able to make great progress on building Navy Town, despite the twice daily visits of the Japanese seaplanes. We had few hits ashore since most of their bombing targets were the ships in the bay, including the Coast Guard transport *Middleton*. She should have been an easy target since she was grounded and could not maneuver during raids and avoid being hit. It was a miracle that

---

1. In January 1943, Japanese aircraft strafed Constantine Harbor on Amchitka Island. *See* also Rigge and the Editors, *War in the Outposts*, 132–133.

no ships were hit despite the constant efforts of the Japanese seaplanes.

One day I went out in a small boat to the *North Coast*, the cargo ship that had brought us over, to arrange for the delivery of materials and supplies needed in our work. I purposely picked the middle of the day for my visit, since I preferred not to be aboard during an air raid. Unfortunately, the Japanese picked that time for a surprise attack on ships in the bay. The crew of the *North Coast* headed for battle stations and the captain assigned me to the bridge. This gave me a grandstand seat for the show. The ship made a slow diversionary movement, while the 20-mm guns aboard made a terrible din, shaking the ship fore and aft. Bombs from the planes dropped all around us, sending up geysers of water. All this was a fascinating sight—just like the movies, except this was far more hazardous. Then one of the Japanese planes dropped a bomb just off our bow and one just off our stern. Frankly, I was scared, since I felt that they had us "pegged" and would get a direct hit on the ship on the next pass. To my surprise and delight, the planes turned around and headed back toward Kiska. Maybe they ran out of bombs. Anyway, the ship and its crew, including me, were spared. I completed arrangements for transfer of materials and supplies to be sent ashore to us. I also took several cases of Hershey chocolate bars that I had brought from Adak for the use of our personnel. These came in handy later to trade to army tractor drivers for road work in our camp. I was happy to be ashore again, since I preferred taking my chances in my foxhole during air raids.

My tent quarters now housed a motley crew. Captain McKenna, my boss from Dutch Harbor, was with us on a short inspection tour; Ensign Jeffus; "Doc" Biggers; a Navy artist, a lieutenant (j.g.) doing oils for the navy; Keith Wheeler, a writer with the *Chicago Daily News*; a CPO (Chief Carpenters Mate) and myself. We were crowded in our tent quarters but got along fine and had fun with each other, despite the miserable weather, poor food and constant air raids. Keith Wheeler was gathering material for a book to be called *The Pacific Is My Beat*. Later, he sent us an autographed copy. Sam Hamill and I were mentioned in this book concerning the episode in Adak with General Landrum and the 6" navy gun traded for a tractor and a trailer. The 4th Seabees

detachment here in Amchitka also got a few pages in his b᷈
Incidentally, Captain McKenna brought official word that I was
a spot Lt. Commander—which meant that I would revert back
to Lieutenant when I was no longer attached to a construction
battalion in a war zone.

Just down the hill from our quarters, just beyond the common
latrine, were the quarters of the [U.S.] Army command: Brigadier
General Jones, Col. Mark Logie, and a captain as an aide. Although
I was now a lieutenant commander, I was sorely outranked by
the army. However, I was never aware of this situation, since
I represented the navy and was treated as an equal.

Lt. Sam Hamill, our communications officer, had set up a shore
to ship blinker on the bluff near our tent quarters. This provided us
with direct communication with ships in the bay. Keith Wheeler,
the writer, assisted in the operation of this signal system. Once,
after an air raid, the *North Coast*, our ship, blinked this message:
"We think our 20-mm gun just shot down a Japanese plane off
Kirilov Point. Please confirm, we are concerned." Keith had this
message blinked back to the North Coast: "Your 20-mm cannon
did not—repeat, did not—shoot down any Japanese plane, but did
wound two army privates in the breakfast mess line ashore—we
are all concerned." As stated earlier, we were all more concerned
about our antiaircraft fire than the Japanese seaplanes.

Later, one night, I awoke with a sudden urge to relieve myself.
I hurried from my tent toward the latrine down the hill. As usual,
it was raining, and I could tell I would never make it to the latrine
in time—so I jumped into the nearest foxhole and relieved myself.
I intended to get up early the next morning to go out and clean
up the mess in the foxhole. Unfortunately, we had an early air
raid warning and all hands headed for their foxholes. Later, I was
walking along the camp with Ensign Jeffus to go over the job plans
for the day. Suddenly, Ensign Jeffus blurted out: "Commander,
some SOB shit in my foxhole last night." I could not contain myself
and broke out in a loud laugh and answered: "Yes I know—you are
looking at him." Just another example of life in the raw on this
Aleutian outpost.

The 4th Seabee Detachment continued work on Navy Town,
consisting primarily of Quonset hut erection for quarters, messing
facilities and administrative functions. We had to knock off work

twice a day due to the Japanese air raids. The army engineers finally completed the short fighter strip in the valley below our camp. At least it was considered operational. It had only taken a few weeks for the job, but it seemed like months to us. The day after the strip was declared usable, six P-40's (Army Air Forces fighter planes) arrived in the middle of the day and quietly landed on the strip! They had carried extra disposable fuel tanks to make the flight from Adak. We were very happy to see them, for now we would have a measure of protection from the Japanese planes on Kiska. We all hoped that Japanese intelligence was not aware of their arrival. Early the following morning our fighter planes took off and went to hide in the clouds above. Soon we heard the Japanese planes coming in on their usual morning raid. Instead of going to our foxholes, we all gathered on the hillside overlooking the strip to witness the fight. It was all over in a few minutes. Our P-40's descended from the clouds above, surprised the Japanese pilots, and shot down four of their planes. They all fell into the bay with their crews. We saw no attempt at bailing out (Japanese pilots never carried parachutes). Two of the Japanese planes got away and hightailed it back toward Kiska. Our fighters lost them in the fog, so we assumed they made it back home. As our fighter planes returned to the strip, we all stood and cheered wildly. You would have thought that this had been a football game—rather than a matter of life and death for human beings. We were paid no more visits from the Japanese, so we were able to concentrate on our mission without the usual interruptions. We were concerned that the Japanese might mount a land assault on Amchitka from Kiska—only 65 miles away—however Colonel Logie assured us that we could hold them if they attempted to land troops on our beaches. I believed him and dismissed my latent fears of that eventuality.

One day later, a major-general from the Alaskan Army Command came to see us from his headquarters in Anchorage. I was requested to attend a meeting to represent the navy as senior naval officer ashore. This senior officer would rule on the division of real estate on Amchitka between the various units on the island. It was amusing that anyone would be concerned about land acquisition on this desolate island. The general asked me to present the navy's request for land for Navy Town. There was no discussion or argument.

The general from Anchorage nodded his approval for my request. Obviously, this army officer felt the need to take care of the navy, though we were sorely outranked: A spot lieutenant commander and a major general.

I was pleased to receive my final approval for the site of Navy Town. I suspect that my friend Colonel Logie[2] paved the way for the major general's approval of my request prior to my arrival at the meeting. Now, we were able to firm our plans for completing Navy Town on the bluff overlooking the bay.

Later I made a courtesy call on the Coast Guard captain who was still aboard his stranded ship on the beach. The captain of the *Middleton* had remained aboard his ship, although the engine room was flooded and he had no heat or lights. He had a small coal stove in his quarters and a Coleman lantern for light. His surroundings were pretty grim. I wondered why he did not move ashore instead of staying with this sitting duck during all the Japanese air raids. I surmised that he was imbued with the "Code of the Sea" and elected to stay with his ship. Fortunately, the air raids had caused no further damage to the ship. He must have suffered mental anguish as he faced a certain investigation for allowing his ship to go around. He graciously offered me supplies and equipment, which we could use in our mission ashore. He was a real gentleman.

A few days after my visit with the captain of the stricken *Middleton*, a key salvage civilian arrived with a tug and a crane barge. His mission was to float the ship and tow it to Seattle for repairs in dry dock. Personally, I felt this was a hopeless task, considering the ship's position in the bay mud and the rugged weather in this unprotected bay at this time of year. However, the civilian had just finished similar salvage jobs at Pearl Harbor on the damaged and sunken [battle] ships brought about by the infamous December 7, [1941] raid by the Japanese—that brought us into this fracas. He was considered the "best in the business." He stayed in our camp and discussed with us his plan to refloat the *Middleton*. He seemed so confident of success that I began to believe he would succeed. In a few weeks, he and his divers put a patch on the

2. Colonel Logie died in Los Gatos, California, in April 1983—his obituary was in the *Retired Officers Association Journal*. [This note was included in the original typed memoir.]

damaged hull, pumped out the hold of the ship, and then with the
help of a real high tide, managed to get the vessel afloat in the
bay. Then, they started the long tow with their tug boat back to
Seattle—a real hazardous journey due to the weather and potential
enemy attack. Adak would be their first stop. We had witnessed a
remarkable ship rescue project. Sometime later, I had the pleasure
of seeing the repaired *Middleton* at a dock in Seattle. She was back
in service as a transport. I never heard whether the captain was
allowed to remain with his ship—I sincerely hope so.

Late in February 1943, about two months after our arrival
on this desolate island, I received a dispatch advising the 4th
Seabee Detachment (50 Seabees) would be relieved by one half
of the 42nd Construction Battalion (about 500 Officers and men).
They would undertake larger projects on the island, including an
airfield, which we had already surveyed on the flat plateau above
the fighter strip. We discounted construction of administrative
facilities and concentrated on quarters and messing facilities for
this larger contingent of Seabees. We worked around the clock to
meet the deadline of their expected arrival. Our small detachment
responded to the task with vigor, since we looked forward to leaving
this bleak environment and returning to the relative luxury of
Dutch Harbor. Also, we would be able to join our former associates
in the 4th Construction Battalion. The half battalion of the 42nd
arrived by navy transport early in March and we had everything
in readiness for them to move right in. I was proud of the job my
50 Seabees had done on short notice. Now we were ready to take
the first available transportation to Dutch Harbor.

On March 9, 1943, I received orders to return to Adak instead
of Dutch Harbor, as I had anticipated. Lt. Cmdr. Neil Kingsley
was now the OINC of the 4th Seabees. He and I had been spot-
promoted to lieutenant commander on the same day. However,
since he was regular navy, he had just received his permanent
rank and took the new date of rank. Now, by a quirk of fate, I was
senior to Neil. The navy is sticky about these things, so I would
not report to someone I was senior to. I was disappointed in not
being able to return to Dutch Harbor, but accepted the decision
"as just one of those things." On March 10, I received detachment orders from the 4th and new orders from the 6th Regiment
in Adak.

## *Adak Island*

My new orders advised that I should report to Cmdr. Roger Hall, Officer-in-Charge of the 6th Construction Regiment at Adak, as executive officer. Earlier, my first skipper, Joe Bronson, had been promoted to OINC of the 1st Seabee Regiment at Dutch Harbor. Soon after, Capt. Robert Meade, another regular officer from the naval academy, had been sent out from Washington as OINC of the First Construction Brigade. We were really making early Seabee history in this Aleutian sector [of the Pacific Theater]. I departed on the first available ship, along with the 4th Seabee Detachment, and debarked at Adak. They continued on to Dutch Harbor.

On arrival at Adak, I reported to Cmdr. Roger Hall as executive of the 6th Seabee Regiment. I had met Roger before and liked and admired him. He was a very successful building contractor in Washington, D.C. They preferred that he stay as a civilian contractor to promote the war effort. I reported to him and was assigned quarters with him in a Quonset hut near our headquarters. The base at Adak had changed considerably since my departure less than three months before. The Seabees had left Navy Town and had built a new area at the end of Sweeper's Cove. Operational personnel and the navy command remained in the original Navy Town. Commander Hall and I "hit it off" from the beginning, so I forgot my original disappointment on not returning to the 4th in Dutch Harbor. It was obvious that Commander Hall was a volunteer, since he was married and engaged in defense construction back in Washington. I had heard previously that he had to exercise some "clout" to persuade the navy to give him a CEC commission under these circumstances.

One of my first assignments after reporting as executive to the 6th Regiment was to prepare for the arrival of Capt. Robert Meade, OINC of the 1st Naval Construction Brigade, with his staff. They were moving out to Adak from Dutch Harbor. No sooner had we got Captain Meade and his staff settled, when we received word that we should prepare facilities for Admiral John ("Jakey") Reeves, the senior naval commander in the Aleutian sector, and his staff. They were moving out to Adak from Kodiak. Obviously, both Dutch Harbor and Kodiak were now considered out of the war zone, so Adak now was getting all the play.

The admiral sent his aide, Cmdr. Herbert Fleishhacker, Jr., to prepare for the move of the flag to Adak. This commander was from San Francisco. His father had donated the zoo (and the famous outdoor pool) that bore his name in that city. "Herb" had a tendency to throw his weight around since he represented the admiral. Despite his constant interference, we proceeded on schedule to set up a satisfactory facility for the commander, Alaskan sector, and his staff. Only one disturbing incident occurred prior to the admiral's arrival in Adak. The box containing his china with the two stars got lost after being unloaded from somewhere on Adak. He thought an army unit had stolen it from the navy dock, where the ship had unloaded the rest of the gear. He envisioned that these army rascals would be feasting on spam from the admiral's china. Everyone, including Captain Hodgskins, the navy base commander, got into the act and wouldn't let go. Since the stevedore unit attached to our regiment had unloaded the ship that brought in the china, I decided to do a little research of my own. I uncovered some "scuttlebutt" that the chief's mess had found some of the fancy china. I could have made an inspection of the chief's mess to follow up on this rumor; however, I decided on another plan. I called the chief commissary steward and CPO in charge of the stevedore unit to report to my office. I told them of the missing china and the concern of the top command. I suggested that the two chiefs conduct a search along the waterfront road, just in case the crate containing the china had fallen off a truck and slid down the bank into the tall grasses, where it would not be readily visible from the road. I was not surprised when the two chiefs came back to my office in a short while to say that my suggestion had paid off. A crate with the missing china had been found.

When the two chief petty officers reported to me that they had found the crate containing the admiral's missing china, I contacted the admiral's aide and arranged for the chiefs to deliver the crate with the china in person to him. He was so relieved and grateful that he offered to suggest that Admiral Reeves send the chiefs a personal letter of thanks for their noble effort in finding the lost china. I told him that this was not necessary and would probably embarrass them, since Seabees are here to serve without praise. Officially, this closed the matter of the missing china; however I had no doubt that these chiefs, with others, had enjoyed eating from the china with two stars, in lieu of the regular aluminum platters. I wondered if the spam or Vienna sausages (our staple meat diet) tasted better from the admiral's china. When I reported the matter and the solution to my regimental commander, he gave me a gracious but knowing smile. I felt that Cmdr. Roger Hall approved of the way I had handled this "ticklish" situation.

The navy transport that brought in the admiral's effects, including the china, also brought Father Smith, the navy chaplain from Dutch Harbor. Lt. Cmdr. Neil Kingsley, OINC of the 4th Seabees, had sent Commander Hall and me a present in the custody of this Catholic priest. The gift was two loaded suitcases filled with bottles of scotch whiskey from the wine mess at Dutch. We all had a drink together (our first in quite a while for me). Then we asked the padre to stay for dinner. We had the usual spam; however, our cook had learned a new way to prepare it—chicken fried! For dessert we had our old standard maraschino cherries (yes, the same ones used in Manhattans). We had cases and more cases of these cherries—and got pretty tired of them. When Father Smith returned to the navy transport, he must have told the captain of the ship of our meager mess. At any rate, Commander Hall and I were invited to have dinner with the captain aboard the transport.

Dinner aboard the navy transport with the line captain was a gourmet meal I won't soon forget. We started with smoked oysters (my first!), steak, French-fried potatoes, a green salad with French dressing, and ice cream for dessert. Compared to the regular fare we had been experiencing, this was really sumptuous. We invited the captain over to our mess for dinner and he came a few days later. He joined Commander Hall and me for a scotch and water, but when Commander Hall insisted on "seconds," the Captain said: "Commander, one is just right, two is too many—and three ain't half enough!" I had not heard this one before. For dinner we had Vienna sausage instead of spam, for a change.

One morning a few days later, I was in my office when a young CEC lieutenant (j.g.) entered and saluted briskly. In the navy one does not wear a cap and salute indoors—the army does. His military manner startled me, since we had long since dispensed with most military courtesies in the Seabees up here in the Aleutians. He told me he had just arrived with the 42nd Seabees

and wished to serve in my office for a few days to get acquainted
with the regiment's mission here. He was from San Francisco
[which my grandfather had last visited as a merchant seaman in
the 1920's] and had been with the Water Department there. He had
also worked on the Hetch Hetchy system. This brought back earlier
memories of my desire to study hydraulics at the University of
California at Berkeley due to the Hetch Hetchy project—which
I considered an engineering marvel in the field of hydraulics.
I enjoyed Lt. (j.g.) Myron Taterians's company very much and we
became good friends—a friendship that would be renewed in San
Francisco after the war.

Later we had a visitor from our bureau in Washington—Capt.
Harry Bolles. It seemed such a long time since I first met him at
Camp Allen in Norfolk, where I reported initially to him, as he
was the exec under Captain Ware. Now he was on Admiral Ben
Moreell's staff at the headquarters of the Bureau of Yards and Docks.
He decided to make an aerial inspection of the facilities we had
completed with the Seabees in Adak. He went out in a coast guard
PBY (amphibious plane). While circling Andrew Lagoon, the site
of the seaplane base, the fog came in and the plane crashed into
the mountain adjacent. All aboard were killed, including Captain
Bolles. It was tragic to lose such a fine CEC officer. He never knew
he had just been promoted to commodore. He would have become
chief of the bureau had he lived. It all seemed such a waste.

Our regiment completed the navy base at Adak and built a
road over the mountains to Andrew Lagoon, where we had built
the Seaplane Base under trying circumstances, since there was
no road there—we had to fly men and materials by PBY. Which
reminds me that Captain McKenna never sent me the commendation suggested by Admiral Reeves just after completion. In the
meantime, we struggled to meet impractical deadlines, and the war
seemed far away. This was all so different from Amchitka.

Then, suddenly, the war came closer. Naval intelligence advised
that a sizeable Japanese fleet had left Tokyo and headed toward
the Aleutians. I wondered if the 6" naval gun we had installed
on the hill overlooking Sweeper's Cove would still shoot. Suddenly,
we felt like sitting ducks on Adak Island. Then our navy task force
appeared in Sweeper's Cove. It consisted of the *Salt Lake City*,
a heavy cruiser, three destroyers ("tin cans") and three small

submarines. They refueled, loaded on ammo and supplies from our navy base, and headed west with orders to seek and destroy the reported Japanese fleet headed in our direction. I felt sad to see this meager task force heading out to intercept an obviously superior enemy task force. They met the enemy and put up a brave fight in what was called the Battle of the Komandorski Islands [March 27, 1943]. A request came for aerial support from Adak. A squadron of B-24 Bombers from the Army Air Force headed out, but soon got lost in the fog. The navy had to send PBY's to guide them back to Adak. So our task force got no air support. Our cruiser, the flag-ship, was hit and was practically dead in the water. Just when it looked like the Japanese fleet would move in for the kill, one of our little subs made a final pass at the Japanese flagship, which sustained some damage from our torpedoes. To the great surprise and relief of our task force, the Japanese fleet left the area and headed back toward Tokyo. Our badly beaten task force limped back into Adak. It was sad to see the dead and wounded on the ships and the terrible damage we had sustained. We will never know why the Japanese fleet did not annihilate our Task Force— and then sail right into Adak.

Just as we were getting settled down after the beating we took at the Komandorskis, we had to slug it out with the two navy captains at the navy base. They continued to demand personal services from our Seabees. We managed to avoid assigning our men as servants to these "clowns" (idiots) until Admiral Reeves arrived and put them in their place. For a while, it was a miser-able job for me to avert the unreasonable demands from these two captains. Now, with support from the commander of the Alaskan sector, Adm. John Reeves, on our side, we were able to concentrate on the rest of our mission at Adak.

Just when things were getting back to normal, we received orders to outfit a transport with Seabees and army personnel headed our way with a mission to take Attu, one of the western-most islands in the Aleutian chain. The new strategy was to bypass Kiska, where the Japanese were entrenched, and cut them off by taking Attu. The Seabees on the transport were detachments from the 12th, 23rd and 22nd Battalions. Most of them were green, with no Aleutian experience. The combat army troops aboard had just come from training in the California desert. It seemed a shame to send these untried people to take Attu. Anyway, they had orders to take anything they might need from our 6th Regiment—and they did. They really robbed us blind, loaded their transport and headed for Attu. I could not understand why army and navy personnel with Aleutian weather experience had not been selected for this hazardous mission. Anyway, I was happy not to be included on this foray—Adak looked pretty good to me just now.

It took a while for the 6th Regiment to be reorganized, after the raid on our equipment and construction materials for the Attu mission. As the executive of the regiment, I spent many weary hours trying to placate the angry battalion commander, who felt crippled by what had happened due to the Attu mission. The trend of events made it increasingly difficult to get the job done. I noted a low point in morale, which had been very high up to now. I was becoming tired and weary just trying to keep the show on the road. Just when things seemed the bleakest for me, there appeared a light at the end of the tunnel.

Just when I felt that I had it up to there and wished I could leave this dreadful place, Captain Meade, our brigade commander, brought me welcome news. He gave me a copy of a letter he had written to Capt. John Perry, detail officer for our bureau. In substance, the letter stated that Lieutenant Commander Ritter had spent almost a year in the Aleutians, was physically tired, and should be returned to the continental United States—and given a Seabee battalion. The letter further stated that I had demonstrated genuine leadership under trying conditions, and despite the fact that I was only a spot lieutenant commander, he felt that I would make a good OINC of a construction battalion. This letter came as a welcome surprise, since I had recently been in the dumps. I had no idea Captain Meade had ever bothered to recognize any talents that I might possess. I was also pleased at the prospect of going home again.

A few days later, I received a commendation letter signed by Captain McKenna at Dutch Harbor. In brief, the letter stated that my performance on Amchitka Island, despite enemy air attacks, and intolerable weather, had been outstanding—and in the best tradition of the Commendable Naval Service. So, when my own morale was at its lowest ebb, these two illustrations of recognition by my superior officers were quite timely.

Cmdr. Bart Gillespie flew over from Kodiak to join the brigade staff here. Adm. Ben Moreell, chief of our bureau in Washington, had requested that Bart go up to the top of Alaska, along the Bering Sea, to evaluate the possibility of oil on a naval reserve in a desolate area above the Arctic Circle. Bart had earlier been engaged in oil exploration back in Texas and was considered well qualified to take the initial observation for oil in this area. He talked to me at great length about this mission, since he knew I was from Houston and had some familiarity with this subject. I was scared that he might discover that I had worked with the Shell Oil Co. in Texas and Louisiana in oil geophysics for several years. He might just insist that I join him on this mission above the Arctic Circle. Our chief would have ordered me to go with Bart had he requested it—so I kept quiet about my Shell Oil experience. Needless to say, I walked a pretty tight rope for several days. I had visions of a delay in my return home. I had no idea how long this outing to the far north would take. Finally, when Bart left without requesting me to go, I felt tremendously relieved. Incidentally, his observations led to the discovery of the vast oil field on the naval reserve, which prompted the Alaskan Pipeline to deliver the oil many years later to Anchorage.

Finally, on May 22, 1943,[3] I received orders to proceed by first available government transportation to Seattle, for further orders to report to Camp Perry at Williamsburg, Virginia. Now, I would be going back home on my way to report to this new Seabee training station—and the prospect of being given a battalion of my own. On May 23, I boarded SS *Toloa*, a navy hospital ship, bound for Dutch Harbor. So, I bade my friends on Adak a fond farewell.

3. The Battle of Attu began on May 11 and ended on May 30, 1943, with 549 Americans and 2,351 Japanese killed. It ended with the Japanese garrison annihilated, as a result of both combat and suicide (largest mass suicide in the war), with only 28 POW's. See also Rigge and the Editors, *War in the Outposts*, 134–141. Attu was the only land battle fought on American soil during World War II. The Aleutian Islands Campaign officially ended on August 15, 1943. After the end of the Aleutian Campaign, from 1943–1945, the U.S. Navy conducted bombing raids from Attu on the Northern Kuril Islands as a diversion, which caused the Japanese Imperial Command to divert about one sixth of their air strength to defend the Northern Kurils from possible invasion. (*Last Flight of Bomber 31*, *Nova*, 2003).

## Aboard the SS Toloa

When I boarded this hospital ship, I was on the first leg of my journey back to Seattle and home. I hated to leave my old friend, Cmdr. Roger Hall, and other good friends I had made in the 6th Regiment and 1st Brigade, but I was happy to leave this miserable weather and desolate land. I walked through the hospital wards on the ship and my heart went out to the patients in their bunks. They were all casualties from the taking of Attu from the Japanese. These were the first evacuees and most of them had bad cases of frozen feet. This confirmed my earlier fears about sending green personnel into this cold Aleutian sector. They were paying for their lack of knowledge of how to take care of themselves in this severe climate. This was a dreary trip to Dutch on this hospital ship. The weather was also miserable. However, we made it safely to Dutch Harbor and docked at the "Ballyhoo" Dock there. All the sights were so familiar. I looked forward to seeing my old buddies in the 4th Seabees, while awaiting further government transportation.

## Dutch Harbor

It was nice to be back after a long absence. I visited with my former comrades in the 4th Seabees, and noted the progress my earlier detachment (Co. A & Co. D) had made in developing army facilities on Unalaska Island. Also, the waterfront work the remainder of the battalion had done at Dutch Harbor was outstanding. I was proud of the accomplishments of the 4th in my absence. Lt. Cmdr. Neil Kingsley showed me around and made me feel like a returning hero—which I wasn't! While walking with him on Dutch, I suddenly saw a woman walking by. I shouted to Neil: "Look Neil, there is a woman." He replied: "Take it easy, Rex. That is the same army nurse that was here when you left us." I had not seen one woman in over six months. This reminded me of a chief petty officer in Amchitka, who told me he had heard that there was a woman behind every tree in the Aleutians. Very true, since there are no trees—which a farm boy from the piney woods of East Texas finds it hard to comprehend. It was with some reluctance that I took my leave from Dutch Harbor, over ten months since my arrival. However, in order to continue my journey to Seattle to follow my basic orders, I arranged a ride on a navy PBY headed for Kodiak.

My officer buddies on Dutch managed to get me pretty drunk on my last night. Around June 1, I departed on the next leg of my journey home.

## Kodiak

As the PBY came into Kodiak for a landing, the view was spectacular. Kodiak is the first island in the long Aleutian chain. It juts out into the Bering Sea and is separated from mainland Alaska by a narrow channel. As we landed, I could see a veritable forest of trees on the mainland. This was a welcome sight after almost a year on the treeless Aleutians. A few officers from the 38th Seabees met our PBY and took me over to their officer's club. They must have noticed how starry-eyed I was in the plush surroundings there. Ensigns Norman Martinsen and Larry Wise were my hosts. Norman was a graduate of the University of Washington at Seattle. Larry was from Stanford University in Palo Alto, California, near San Francisco. They gave me the returning hero treatment, since they knew of my experience in the war zone area of the Aleutians. They were very interested in Adak, since their battalion would be going there soon. I expected that Norman would inherit my old job there as exec of the 6th Regiment.

Their battalion bar fascinated me. The walls were covered with oil paintings by their battalion artist. The paintings all carried the motif of the Robert W. Service poem about the Yukon. I shall never forget the one directly above the bar—a wild and gray character, with bushy hair, and long boney fingers on the keys of a piano. Underneath, was the inscription: "My God, how that man could play." Very, very, clever and expressive.

They took me to very plush quarters in their BOQ. Now I know how naval officers are supposed to live—a far cry from my quarters in Amchitka! Next day they took me on a tour of Kodiak. Here was a complete navy base. I also saw the *Yale* tied up to a dock in the harbor. I had often seen the *Yale* and its sister ship the *Harvard* in San Francisco, when I was in the Merchant Marine. They were based there and were coastal cruise ships that went to San Pedro, San Diego and Seattle. Now they had been mustered into the navy. My friends also took me over to the mainland, with beautiful scenery and forests of trees. I felt like I was back home in East Texas. My stay in Kodiak was short, but very pleasant.

This is one spot in the Aleutians I would welcome returning to—which is more than I can say about places further west on the chain. Later they took me back to the airport, where I boarded a Pan-American DC-3, under charter to the navy. The DC-3 was considered the workhorse for the services due to its dependability. Compared with my other flights, this was really plush transportation. This flight would take me to Seattle, with a stop in Anchorage.

## Anchorage, Alaska

Our Pan Am DC-3 landed in Anchorage, where we would spend the night. Before proceeding on to Seattle, I was met at the airport by a navy line commander, who escorted me to the BOQ. I was really getting VIP treatment since I left Adak on way to Seattle. The commander suggested that we eat out, rather than having dinner at the "closed" mess in the BOQ. He took me to Aunt Dinah's place, where the specialty of the house was southern fried chicken. Aunt Dinah was a black lady, obviously from the Deep South. The chicken was great. I had not had fried chicken in many months. We also attended a floor show following the dinner. Around midnight, I suggested we return to the BOQ for some sleep, since I had an early flight in the morning. It seemed that I had hardly hit the sack when I was roused to catch my DC-3. I could not believe it was daylight, since my watch showed 0230. I had forgotten the long days this far north as we approached the summer solstice (June 21). We had a smooth take-off and our next stop would be Seattle.

## Over the Inside Passage

Our flight took us over the Inside Passage, through which our ship had detoured on the way up to Dutch Harbor (back in June 1942). We flew low over Ketchican, which is the north end of the Inside Passage. We also had a good look at Sitka. Fortunately, there was no fog and the view from the plane was magnificent. Our pilot flew very low down the passage, which gave me some wonderful views of this spectacular area. As I flew down this waterway, my hope was to be able to take a cruise ship on this passage (I did, 34 years later, in 1977). We had a good view of Vancouver, British Columbia, at the end of the Passage. We saw the famous bridge over the ship channel [built in 1939]. Later, I got a good look at Bellingham, Washington, which brought back memories of unloading lumber here on the SS *Vinita* back in 1925, when I was in the Merchant Marine with my college buddy Tommie Ward. We had a smooth landing in Seattle. Now, I felt like I was back home—the Aleutians seemed far, far away.

# Chapter 3

✦
✦
✦
✦
✦

# 1943: Back to the States

## *Seattle*

On my arrival at Seattle on May 31, 1943, I reported to DIRALDOCKS (Director, Alaskan Bureau of Yards & Docks). The director was Rear Admiral Carl Trexel. He was from Iowa and had gone to Iowa State. Although he was regular navy (a career officer in the Civil Engineer Corps), he had not attended the Naval Academy. In other words—he was not a "trade school" boy. I liked him instinctively from the beginning. Our friendship continued until his death in San Francisco many years later. My reception at this office was quite different than the one we had received on our way out to Dutch Harbor. Admiral Trexel was a great admirer of the Seabees— which is more than you could say for his predecessor.

To my surprise, and delight, the admiral suggested that I take some leave and go to Houston to see my folks before reporting to Camp Perry at Williamsburg, Virginia, my next duty station. I registered in a downtown hotel and, after dinner, I took a short stroll down the street. I passed a theater which was playing *Porgy and Bess*, the musical comedy [probably the closest thing to American opera] composed by George Gershwin [who had died in 1937]. I had never seen the show, though I had heard the music many times and remembered the melodies fondly, especially "Summer Time." I was fortunate to obtain a seat for the show. I went in and thoroughly enjoyed it. This was truly a welcome home for a "refugee" from the Aleutians. The singing reminded me of the black women singing in the "True Vine" church on Uncle Jim Ritter's place in Buncombe, Texas, near Murvaul—where I grew up.[1]

Next morning I reported to Admiral Trexel. He had arranged leave papers, pay day and even gas coupons for my use at my folks' home. His office gave me the air tickets to Camp Perry, Virginia, via Houston, and had already made reservations for a flight to Houston a couple of days later. I really enjoyed the contacts with this friendly and efficient office. This gave me a far better feeling about the navy than I previously held. On my way to the airport, I passed a ship tied up at the dock. I was really happy to recognize the *Middleton*, the Coast Guard ship that was aground at Amchitka. I hoped the captain was still aboard.

## *Rosenberg, Texas*

When I arrived at the Houston airport, Dad and Mama met me in the Buick Special automobile, which I had left with him over a year ago. It was great to see my parents again after a year in the Aleutians. We drove from the airport to Rosenberg, about 20 miles distant. They had moved from their Gulf Pipe Line Station in Almeda, Texas, and had rented a house in Rosenberg, next door to my sister, Lois. Dad was now working as a pumper for the Gulf Oil Company at Thompson, a few miles away.

A few days after arriving home, I decided to drive into Houston to visit friends. I told dad about the gas ration coupons[2] the navy had issued me in Seattle. He said "You won't need these. Just drive to our filling station and tell them 'to fill her up.'" You see, gas rationing had not reached their town yet. While in Houston, I dropped by Battlestein's, a men's clothing store, and bought a new uniform. This was the newly authorized

1. "Uncle" Jim Ritter was the father of the famous cowboy singer Tex Ritter (1905–1974), who was Rex's first cousin and life-long friend.

2. My grandmother saved some of her wartime gas ration coupons, which are still in the family World War II collection. Wartime gas rationing was the hardest thing for the Office of Price Administration (OPA), which was in charge of rationing, to enforce on the home front.

uniform with shoulder boards rather than sleeve braid to indi-
cate rank. This was a beautiful blue-gray uniform and I felt
proud to wear it. It was a relief to get out of the standard blues,
since it was hot and humid there. Unfortunately, this uniform
did not catch on in the navy and was dropped soon afterward.
The regulars felt it made us look like postmen. I was sorry to
see it discontinued. After the war, Jeannette had a beautiful suit
made from the uniform material.

My parents drove up to East Texas with me to visit relatives and
friends. I could tell that my dad wanted to show me off in Gary
and Carthage. To him, I was a returning hero—which I considered
an exaggeration. I enjoyed our visit with relatives and friends—
especially Grandma Templin. She had lived with us while I was
growing up in Murvaul and Gary. She always said I was her favorite
grandson—which pleased me. She was over 90 now, but was very
alert. She knew about Sherman's [1864] March to the Sea during
the Civil War. As a girl, she grew up in Holly Springs, Mississippi.
I was anxious to hear her version of events during that period.
Instead, Grandma wanted to talk about my experiences in
the Aleutians and how long I thought it would take to whip the
Japanese. She read the *Houston Chronicle* every day and knew
more about the progress of World War II than I did. When I insisted
that she recall Sherman's raid, where his soldiers burned their
barns and stole their livestock, she just smiled and said: "Son,
they say that Sherman said 'War is hell'—my folks felt that Sherman
was hell."[3] It was good to have this visit with her, Aunt Eliza, Uncle
George and their children, but I could not stay long, since I would
have to leave Houston for my next duty station.

We drove back to Rosenberg, and the next day, Dad and Mama
drove me to the airport to catch a plane on my way to Camp
Perry. I had no illusions of returning soon, since I felt that this
war would last quite a while and I expected to go overseas again
with the Seabees.

## Camp Peary, Virginia

I reported to Camp Perry on June 18, 1943. This new Seabee
training center is only six miles from Williamsburg, the historic

3. After the end of the war in 1945, President Harry Truman said that
"Sherman was wrong. Peace is hell." (*Truman, American Experience*, 1997)

colonial town that was restored by the Rockefeller Family. My friend, Clyde Trudell, whom I met in Dutch Harbor, who was with the 21st Battalion, had worked as an architect in developing the restoration project [which was ahead of its time when it began in the late 1920's]. This new base superseded the old Camp Allen, where I originally reported [back in April 1942]. Capt. James Ware was the commanding officer here as he had been at Camp Allen at the Norfolk Naval Base. Howard ("Shag") Ransford, who was training officer at Camp Allen, was the executive officer at this Seabee training center.

On arrival here, I was assigned to Area E, humorously called "Bots Town." This area was basically intended for officers reporting for initial duty—not for veteran officers like me. They had roll calls at ungodly hours in the morning. It did not take me long to find out how to avoid these. I spent many pleasant hours in Williamsburg and had several dinners at the Inn to escape navy fare at the officers' mess. The Rockefellers did a fine restoration job here to make you feel transplanted into colonial days. It is a fascinating place to visit—even now!

Although I managed to avoid the early roll calls, I was not so lucky in regard to the Obstacle Course. They insisted that I complete this strenuous training course conducted by a rough marine sergeant. Although the course was rough, I was still in good shape, thanks to my Aleutian experience. I finished the Obstacle Course and got my certificate. Then I found out that due to my age (40) and a year's duty in the war zone, I should have been excused. Anyway, I was glad I took the course and passed, just to prove that I was still physically fit.

Since I had no regular duty assignment, I spent a lot of time in Commander Ransford's office, where I assisted in selecting personnel for battalions being formed. Apparently, my year in the war zone gave some credence to my judgment in personnel selections for these new Seabee battalions. "Shag" Ransford seemed to like having me around and trusted my judgment on selection matters. He tried hard to inveigle me to take a station billet and work with him for newly formed battalions. However, I held out on the premise that I had been promised command of a battalion on my departure from Adak.

Later, "Shag" asked me to take over command of an area with all black Seabees undergoing boot training. Most of the enlisted personnel in this area were draftees—better known as "hand-cuffed volunteers." All the earlier Seabees I had known were real volunteers, but lately the navy had been forced, against its will, to accept a quota of draftees for these later Seabee battalions. "Shag" figured that with my farm background in Texas and association with blacks, I would be a logical choice to ride herd on these new black arrivals. I explained that though I had grown up with blacks, I had not worked with any since I left the farm to go to college. To my delight and surprise, he agreed to let me off the hook, with some reluctance. I knew, of course, that he could have ordered me to this duty, so I duly appreciated his action in this matter.

Frequently I would go down to the railroad station on the base and watch the new arrivals, straight from civilian life, debark from the train to start a new life with the Seabees. Usually, there was an "unofficial" greeting committee on hand to welcome the new recruits. The standard greeting was: "You'll be sorry." One day a train arrived with new draftees from South Carolina. It seems that a young black man got aboard this troop train at his hometown in South Carolina to say goodbye to some of his friends. He had not been drafted yet. When he tried to leave the train, just as they were pulling out, the master-at-arms in charge of the group restrained him—he figured he was trying to desert. The victim was unable to convince the petty officer in charge of the train that he was being "Shanghaied." He was kept on the train until they arrived at Camp Perry. At the base he kept insisting that he did not belong with the group, but was being shoved along with the usual routine of arrivals. Finally, after receiving most of the shots, he was able to convince a medical officer that he should not be here. This created a problem for the command. Commander Ransford asked me to go see the young man and try to persuade him to enlist. In that way, the navy would be off the hook. He would have no part of this, insisting that he had been forcibly detained all the way from his hometown in South Carolina. Finally, I got him to agree that if we gave him a train ticket back he would forget the whole incident. "Shag" Ransford was relieved by the way I had handled this delicate matter. Incidentally, we assumed he got safely home, since we never heard from him again. I often wondered what kind of Seabee he would have made.

Drew Pearson, the infamous Washington columnist [in the 1930's–1940's], wrote an article accusing Captain Ware of raising pigs on the base using station garbage and selling them for personal gain. All who knew the captain were sure these charges were false; however, the captain held many mess meetings to explain the facts (the pigs were donated to our galleys and station barbecues at no cost). Some tended to believe Drew Pearson. An investigation in Washington verified Captain Ware's version. He sued Pearson and received a cash settlement from the newspaper syndicate. So, finally Captain Ware did make a profit on the pigs!

I continued to work with Commander Ransford on miscellaneous assignments as the weeks went by. Then, on July 10, 1943, we received a message whereby BUDOCKS requested BUPERS to detach me from Camp Perry on July 17, with the orders as to report as OINC (Officer in Charge) of the 107th Construction Battalion. After almost a month at Camp Perry, I was now about to get the duty assignment I came for and was promised. It would appear that Captain Robert Meade's letter from Adak to Captain John Perry requesting that I be given a battalion finally paid off. Since I was only a spot lieutenant commander and was not now in the war zone, I could have been returned to lieutenant rank, and it would have been logical to assign a permanent lieutenant commander to command of a battalion—who could then be the spot promoted to commander when entering a war zone. This action on the part of BUDOCKS confirmed the fact that the Civil Engineer Corps of the navy is a close-knit family and that the personal touch paid off.

There was one minor hitch to my final selection as skipper of the 107th Seabees. Now OINC's and EXEC's for the later battalions were required to be interviewed by the station psychiatrist prior to official assignment. There had been a few sad experiences in earlier battalions with officers in command. For instance, the skipper of the 8th Seabees at Dutch Harbor went off his rocker and had to be returned to the States. Anticipation of my impending visit to the psychiatrist to determine my mental stability was a source of concern. However, I duly reported to the "shrink's" office for my interview. As I entered the outer office, I met Lt. Howard McKay, who was there to pass the screening for executive officer of the 107th. It was our first meeting and the beginning of a team to operate the affairs of this battalion for the foreseeable future. Fortunately, we both passed the psychiatric test (my first), thereby clearing the last hurdle for being assigned to the battalion.

I received orders signed by Cmdr. Howard Ransford, dated July 13, 1943, for the 107th Construction Battalion in area B-7 of Camp Perry, with a departure date of July 24 for Camp Endicott, Davisville, Rhode Island. Lt. McKay and I worked feverishly with the assigned CEC Officers to complete the formation of the battalion. On July 19, I received orders to move the 107th (26 officers & 1081 enlisted men)[4] from Camp Perry to Camp Endicott on July 24, 1943. I also received my basic orders to report for duty as OINC of the 107th Construction Battalion. It was now official. There was no turning back.

The last few days at Camp Perry were hectic, making final arrangements to depart and saying goodbye to old friends, such as Capt. Jimmie Ware and Cmdr. "Shag" Ransford. I had known both since I first reported for active duty at Camp Allen, Norfolk, over a year ago. Up to now, everything had gone smoothly; however, as skipper I suddenly had to face up to a couple of problems. Two young ensigns in the 107th came to request permission to drive up to Davisville (Camp Endicott) with their wives. I noted that one of these wives was from Texas, so I told her that she needed her husband, Ens. Phil Atkins, less for the trip than the troops on our train did. I told him I knew a "Texas" lady would make the trip fine without him and that she and the other ensigns' wives would probably have rooms rented at our new station by the time we got there by train. My prediction came true, so I felt no remorse in requiring the ensigns to accompany the troops on our train.

The second trouble involved a chief petty officer, J.B. Trussell, assigned to the 107th. He was a former school teacher from Hillsboro Texas (just north of Waco). I was familiar with his town, since Hill County was in my territory when I was Project Engineer, Texas State Highway Department, at Waco back in the 1930's. He had heard "scuttlebutt" (rumors) that another battalion being formed at Camp Perry would be going to Gulfport, Mississippi. He asked for a transfer so he and his wife would be closer to Texas. I told him that I could not conceive of one Texan letting another down—since I needed him as chief master-at-arms to head up

---

4. By 1945 there were over 1,000 officers and men in the 107th Battalion.

security in the 107th. He agreed and withdrew his request. This all turned out fine since "Trus" had the necessary patience for this difficult job. He was immediately dubbed "Sheriff" by the others in the battalion. So, I came through my first two tests as skipper of a Seabee unit.

## En Route to Camp Endicott

On July 24, 1943, the officers and men of the 107th Seabees boarded two troop trains and departed from Camp Peary and headed north to Camp Endicott at Davisville, Rhode Island. My train proceeded slowly through Virginia, past Richmond and Alexandria. We passed through Washington, D.C. after dark. This was an all-coach train—no Pullmans—and no air conditioning. The weather was hot and humid and our coal burning engine covered everything with soot. It was not a pleasant ride. Fortunately, it was not a long journey. My seatmate was Lt. Howard McKay, my executive officer. He hailed from Philadelphia. I looked out the window and noted that we were standing in an underground station. On the station platform, opposite our window, I saw one lone spectator—a black WAC. I turned to Mac and said: "So this is your home town—wake me up when we reach New York."

## Camp Endicott, Rhode Island

Early in the morning of July 25, 1943, we pulled into the railroad station at Camp Endicott. We were weary and tired from the long and hot ride on this troop train, but were happy to be on our own at last in a new Seabee base. Camp Endicott is located in Davisville, Rhode Island, about 16 miles from Providence and about two miles from East Greenwich. The Seabee base here is adjacent to Quonset Point Naval Air Station. Newport, the famous resort for the rich [since the Gilded Age after the Civil War], is about 30 miles south, on Long Island Sound. The Naval Officers' Cadet School is located in Newport. Camp Endicott is the Advance Training Seabee Base for the East Coast. Gulfport, Mississippi, is the location for the advance base on the Gulf Coast, and Port Hueneme, California (60 miles north of Los Angeles) is the West Coast construction battalion center for advance training. Since the 107th Construction Battalion was sent here, we assumed that we might be sent to the

European sector [European Theater of Operations (ETO)] for our first overseas assignment. That would suit us just fine.

Camp Endicott was under the command of Capt. Fred Rogers. The base was geared to provide final advance training to new construction battalions before being sent overseas. Everything here was well organized—a far cry from Camp Peary which we had just left. The base was well equipped with essential facilities, such as ships' stores, barber shops, navy exchanges, library and neat mess halls. Our officers and men were delighted with our new surroundings. We were quickly established in our new quarters and our battalion organization was formed in short order. We were essentially on our own and enjoyed this degree of independence. We concentrated on marching and military drills under the direction of our own officers and chief petty officers in anticipation of being reviewed and officially commissioned. We had good public transportation to Providence. I went into Providence quite often in the evenings. I usually ended up at the Biltmore Hotel, with its pleasant cocktail lounge and excellent floor shows. This was a welcome relief from the day to day responsibilities as skipper of a Seabee battalion. Providence was a very pleasant city to visit.

On July 31, 1943, RADM Lewis Combs arrived from BUDOCKS at Washington to conduct a review of the 107th Construction Battalion. He was the Asst. Chief of the Bureau of Yards & Docks, under Adm. Ben Moreell. His lovely wife came with him. Next day, he conducted his official review. To me, it was a fine sight to see all my officers and men suited out in dress whites for this ceremony.[5] After we passed in review, Mrs. Combs presented me with the colors and our battalion flag. These would be with us for the duration of the war. Rear Admiral Combs personally complimented me on the quality of our military drill as we passed in review. In his commissioning speech, he stressed the point that we were not marines or sailors—but Seabees, a proud new addition to the United States Navy. This gave us a real sense of pride to be part of this new addition to the navy. Now, we were an official battalion in training for an overseas assignment.

5. The official commissioning ceremony of the 107th Seabees was the only time during the war that my grandfather wore dress summer whites.

## Sun Valley, Rhode Island

Soon after our commissioning, we moved the 107th Battalion to Sun Valley, only a few miles from Camp Endicott. We were completely on our own at this location. We lived in Quonset huts and had to subsist on our own. This was good training for any new battalion. This brought back memories of similar experiences in the 4th Seabees, when we left Camp Allen and moved to Camp Bradford before going overseas—the Aleutians. This area was part of Camp Endicott and geared primarily to military training. Our military training was based on the premise that we would not be used in combat, except to protect and defend the facilities we had built on "Island X" in the war zone. Enlisted personnel were taught to use carbines and machine guns. The officers, including myself, were sent to the pistol range. I never really cared for the .45 [semi] automatic, but I did pass the course. I much preferred the carbine, but officers were issued the .45 automatics (Colts).[6] Our instructor on the pistol range was Commander Diechler—"hold and squeeze" Diechler— which is what we called him, since that was the way to shoot a .45, rather than just pull the trigger. He emphasized that the primary reason for an officer to have the .45 automatic was to shoot his own men in case of mutiny. Somehow, I abhorred this philosophy. Diechler also stressed the idea that one should never point a pistol at a person except when he intended to kill him—"and then kill him!" he would always add.

He was openly envious of me, since I was only a lieutenant commander and was taking a battalion overseas, while he, a commander, was stuck here on station force. He felt that this was quite unfair. Later, he was detached from station force and given his own battalion. While stationed in Okinawa, he began to drink heavily. One of his junior officers walked into his tent to ask him to come to the officers' mess where the other officers were waiting to have dinner. Apparently, he was surprised when he looked up and saw this junior officer at the door of his tent. He grabbed his .45 automatic pistol and shot the young man in the stomach. Then, realizing what he had done, he placed the gun to his own temple

6. The Model 1911 Colt .45 was standard issue for the U.S. Armed Forces from 1911–1986.

and blew his brains out. The young officer recovered and I saw him several times after the war in San Francisco. This is how I came by this story. Perhaps they forgot to send him to a shrink before giving him a battalion—or perhaps he succumbed to his indoctrination that he gave us on the pistol range.

## Washington, D.C.

On August 8, 1943, I received orders to report to BUDOCKS in Washington for final indoctrination for overseas duty. I looked forward to going to our main office to find out the type of overseas duty that was in store for the 107th. However, I was concerned about the possibility of losing the battalion since I was only a spot lieutenant commander. I had become so attached to the officers and men in the 107th that it would be a crushing blow to lose this battalion.

At BUDOCKS, I was given the word on what to expect on overseas duty [in 1944]. This all seemed superfluous to me, since I had already spent a year in the Aleutians—most of it in the war zone. After his briefing, I was ushered into Rear Admiral Combs' (Asst. Chief of BUDOCKS) office for information on our destination. Capt. John Perry, Bureau Detail Officer, and a couple of other officers were present. I was disappointed to find that we would not be going to the European Area (probably Britain, Sicily or North Africa), as anticipated, but would be going to Camp Parks in California, near Oakland [and San Francisco]—and then to Port Hueneme, near Los Angeles, prior to going overseas in the Pacific Area.

After receiving the information regarding the destination of my battalion, I was told to report to a commander in an adjacent office where I would be "spot" promoted to commander. Rear Admiral Combs explained that recent experiences in overseas locations had indicated that OINC'S of battalions should have the rank of commander. I explained that I was only a spot lieutenant commander and wondered if they could put a spot on the spot. This statement obviously created some dismay on their part. It was as if I had thrown a bombshell at this group of high ranking bureau officers. I had visions of losing my battalion.

My spot lieutenant commander rank obviously presented quite a problem to Admiral Combs and his staff. I could feel his concern about the difficulty of making me a spot commander. I sat quietly by while the problem was being discussed. Then I asked permission to speak to Captain Perry, a former Texan from Waco and an Annapolis graduate, who was now the Detail Officer at BUDOCKS. I made the following suggestion: "Sir, you might consider saving this rank of commander for some other deserving officer. If you will let me keep the 107th Battalion, I promise not to let our bureau down. I am sure I will get along overseas even though I may be occasionally outranked, as I was at times by the army in the Aleutians." Captain Perry replied: "Ritter, I believe you deserve this chance and I recommend that you be retained as OINC of the 107th." Then he addressed Rear Admiral Combs and the other officers present: "Gentlemen, Ritter will likely receive his regular promotion to lieutenant commander before he leaves the country for overseas duty. Then we can spot promote him to commander." Rear Admiral Combs nodded his acceptance and I breathed a deep sigh of relief. I had come so close to losing my battalion until this fellow Texan came to my rescue. I am sure Captain Perry was strongly influenced by Captain Mead's letter from Adak highly recommending me for a command. I was firmly convinced that the personal touch was an overriding factor in our bureau. Now I could return to Camp Endicott and prepare my battalion for a trek to the West Coast. Before I left Washington, I was told to give all the personnel in our battalion ten days leave before departing for California.

## Camp Endicott

I arrived back in Camp Endicott on August 19, 1943, weary but happy to keep my battalion. We arranged ten days leave for all our personnel before departing for the West Coast. I took this opportunity to make a quick trip back home for a few days' visit with my parents in Rosenberg. From Houston, I flew to Dallas and spent the night in the old Adolphus Hotel, where I had spent many pleasant hours before the war. Since I would be spending the next night, hopefully, in New York City,[7] I asked the manager of the Adolphus if he had any influence in getting me a room there for one night.

7. New York City was the main embarkation port for the European Theater of Operations (ETO) on the East Coast, which was dramatized in the 1944 wartime Broadway musical *On the Town* and the 1945 romantic film *The Clock*, with Judy Garland (her only non-singing role at MGM). When Japan surrendered, New York was the site of the biggest VJ Day celebration in the country and the famous VJ photo of the sailor kissing the nurse in Times Square.

Hotel rooms were hard to come by during this period [because of wartime crowding due to military personnel staying in hotels from New York to San Francisco]. He told me to go to the New Yorker in Manhattan, adjacent to Madison Square Garden, and tell the manager there that he had sent me. This worked like a charm— I got a nice room there, with a view. I have always returned to this hotel when in New York—out of appreciation. I spent the next day in the city and then caught a late train for Providence.

On August 27, 1943, I received orders to transfer the 107th Construction Battalion to Camp Parks in Pleasanton, California, east of Oakland. Now, I was able to tell the officers and men of the battalion that we would be going to the Pacific area, not to Europe, as we had anticipated. The last days at Camp Endicott went smoothly and quickly. The day before we were due to depart for the West Coast, I went to a small inn in East Greenwich, Rhode Island, near the base, to try to place a long distance call to my mother in Texas. During this period, getting a line for a long distance call was a real project. I waited my turn for several hours. There were several railroad men present in the bar at this inn. They would not allow me to buy a drink. This was quite a shock to a Southerner, who had grown up feeling that New Englanders were inhospitable—"blue noses," we called them. Anyway, these "Yankees" would not allow this Texan in uniform to buy a drink while I waited for a long distance line to Texas. Finally, I was able to get my call through, and I was still sober enough to talk to my folks and tell them where I was moving to—the West Coast, near San Francisco. I will always remember this pleasant afternoon in East Greenwich, Rhode Island, and would like to return someday and buy the railroad men a drink at the bar at the quaint inn. On September 4, 1943 [the day after the beginning of the Allied invasion of Italy—the first Allied landing in mainland Europe before D-Day], we said goodbye to the many nice people we had met here, including Capt. Fred Rogers. We boarded two Pullman trains for our trip.

## *En Route to Camp Parks*

One of my company officers was train commander on the Pullman train on which I had a stateroom. This time, I could enjoy the trip and let the train commander do the worrying—as I had done on my previous trip [in 1942] to the West Coast with the 4th Battalion. We departed on September 4 and headed west along a northern route for Camp Parks. We crossed the Hudson near Albany, went by Buffalo, but did not see Niagara Falls, passed south of Chicago and went through St. Louis—my first view of this city. We passed through Salina, Kansas, about midday and had a pleasant sunrise. A nice group of ladies came aboard our train with doughnuts, cookies and hot coffee. It seems that this is the custom of Salina to welcome all troop trains that passed through their city. This was the first time this had happened to me. Later, we changed to the Western Pacific lines and passed through Denver, Salt Lake City, Sacramento and Stockton. We arrived at Camp Parks, just west of Livermore and next door to Pleasanton, California, early on September 9. Tired and weary from the long train ride, the personnel of the 107th debarked from the train and headed for Redwood Barracks to which we were assigned.

# Chapter 4

✦
✦
✦
✦
✦

# 1943–1944: Shore Leave

## *Camp Parks and San Francisco— September–November 1943*

This new duty station was part of a larger navy base with a hospital and regular naval units. It is located about 20 miles east of Oakland on Highway 50, which connects Oakland with Tracy and Stockton. The quarters in the Redwood Barracks were comfortable but the weather was hot and dusty. I reported to RADM Norman Smith, an old-time Naval Academy graduate, who had been recalled to active duty. He was obviously unhappy with this assignment. He would have preferred a ship instead of playing nursemaid to the Seabees. Although we were not supposed to do any construction work for the navy in the continental USA, we were immediately assigned the job of erecting Quonset huts at Camp Parks to house other battalions expected soon.

The command got away with this assignment with the guise that this was only training for our Seabees. We were given deadlines to meet in anticipation of expected arrivals of more Seabees. This was good for our personnel. It gave them a chance to work with their hands. After all, they were formerly construction men in civilian life. This was also good practice for the job we would be doing overseas.

This assignment was also a welcome relief from the military training phase we had just been through at Sun Valley, Rhode Island.

We were able to set up a liberal liberty schedule for our officers and men. However, getting to Oakland or San Francisco for the night off was a problem due to the lack of public transportation. Greyhound buses came near by the station along Highway 50, not far from the Main Gate, but rarely stopped. They were always filled. Officers and men had to resort to hitchhiking a ride. Fortunately, the people traveling along Highway 50 were very gracious about picking up our personnel in uniform and dropping them off at the East Terminal of the AC Transit Line, east of Oakland. From here, our people could reach downtown Oakland—and also San Francisco. I discovered that Camp Parks had formerly run navy buses from the base to the AC terminal, but had discontinued this service because of complaints from Greyhound citing unfair competition with a registered carrier. When I pointed out the problem of boarding Greyhound buses, which were usually filled by the time they got to the base, and the lack of service they were providing, they reluctantly restored the navy bus service to the East Bay Terminal. Now, our people had no difficulty getting to either Oakland or San Francisco on liberty. I wondered why the command had not observed this transportation problem and corrected it earlier, without pressure from us. Our people enjoyed getting into the two cities without having to thumb a ride, as they had done earlier. It was pleasant to have this outlet after a hard day's work erecting Quonset huts.

The large hotels in Oakland and San Francisco had a convenient arrangement for officers on liberty to spend the night. Since it was next to impossible to obtain a room in these hotels during this wartime period, they had set up officer dormitories in larger spaces normally used for show rooms and banquet halls. They rented beds in these dorms to officers at very reasonable prices. There always seemed to be room here, even on short notice. Thus, I was always assured of a place to sleep when I chose to stay overnight— which I did frequently to get away from the pressures of running a battalion. In this way, I was able to relax and think problems out.[1]

1. During the war San Francisco was the main embarkation port for the Pacific Theater on the West Coast. In October 1943 the *Saturday Evening Post*

Early in October 1943, I received orders to send the whole battalion on a 25-mile hike to Mount Diablo,[2] near Walnut Creek. Incidentally, Walnut Creek was home to my old skipper, Joe Bronson, in the 4th Seabees. This hike was a long, hot and dusty trek for our troops. I rode up in a jeep and joined them later at the bivouac area. They had made the first 22 miles in less than six hours, but the last three miles up the steep mountain slope slowed them down a bit. They set up pup tents and spent the night, after feasting on K rations for supper. The following morning, they broke camp at the top of Mount Diablo and hiked back to Camp Parks. On their way down the slope of the mountain, one of them found the horned skull of a cow, whitened by the elements, but still retaining a wisp of hair over one eye socket. Later, in a formal ceremony, they presented "Veronica" to me with adoption papers. The name Veronica was chosen due to the wisp of hair over one eye similar to the hair style of Veronica Lake, a current favorite [Hollywood] movie actress. I think my being from Texas inspired the gift. Anyway, Veronica was always accorded a prominent spot behind my desk wherever we were. She became a sort of battalion mascot—a California cow for a Texas cowboy [the frontispiece in this book is a photo of Veronica behind my grandfather's desk when he was on Tinian].

Our battalion band, under the direction of Bandmaster Reid in Headquarters Company, really bloomed at Camp Parks. He whipped these talented musicians into an excellent musical group. He also developed a swing orchestra that played for dances at the base. One night, the orchestra put on a very good show at the base theater with music, magic acts and clever skits. The 107th was

---

ran an ad titled "Don't come to San Francisco Now" to discourage people who were not in the military or working in the defense industry to visit the city until after the war, because of the wartime overcrowding. The late California historian Kevin Starr wrote that "In general terms, the Bay Area and Northern California were army country during World War II, while Southern California belonged to the Navy and Marine Corps. Although this distinction has some validity, the Navy was significantly present in the Bay Area as well." Kevin Starr, *Embattled Dreams: California in War and Peace, 1940–1950*, California Dream series (New York: Oxford University Press, 2002.)

2. There is a beacon on Mount Diablo which is lit on every Pearl Harbor Remembrance Day since 1964, at the request of Admiral Nimitz.

developing a unique character and received favorable attention from the base command.

Based on my earlier experience with the Seabees in the Aleutians, I concluded that the best thing I could do for my battalion was to provide good food and good mail service to maintain high morale. At Camp Parks, I was able to make some good "trades" for people in the Station Force here. I managed to get a fine chief steward to head up our messes. I persuaded a Frenchman named Rene, an excellent baker, to leave Station Force and join the 107th. I also found two mailmen, who had been just that in civilian life, who agreed to come with us. I also managed to swap a warrant officer who was giving us trouble for one in the Station Force I had known previously in the 4th Seabees. McDonald was his name. He had worked previously for the New York State Highway Department. His home was in Rochester. He proved to be a great asset to us, as I predicted, in our Headquarters Company. With trades like these, I was able to improve the quality of our personnel and get the battalion ready for overseas duty in the war zone. Once I obtained permission from the exec at Camp Parks, I had no difficulty in recruiting competent station force personnel to come with us. Also, we had people in the battalion who were afraid to go into the war zone and preferred to be transferred to station force here at Camp Parks.

One day, my old skipper, "Jumping Joe" Bronson from the 4th Seabees, arrived at Camp Parks. He was here on a physical training kick (exercise) they were putting older officers through upon return from overseas duty. Also, Ordiss Forbess, the former Co. B Commander in the 5th Seabees, showed up on his way to a new assignment. I enjoyed visits with these two at the club on the base, where we relived Aleutian days. Forbess was a Texan from Texas Tech.

Around the middle of October 1943, I received a telegram from "Tex" Ritter (1905–1974), my singing cowboy cousin. The telegram stated that he would shortly be doing a show at the Orpheum Theater in Oakland and would be staying at the Leamington Hotel. He asked me to join him there on a designated evening. Obviously, he had gotten my Camp Parks address from my mother. On this evening, Ordiss Forbess and I met Tex at his hotel and went to the theater as his guests. We then returned to his hotel with him to go out to dinner. On our return to the Leamington Hotel, Tex told me he had invited Julia Ross (formerly Julia Adams, his cousin from Carthage, Texas) and her husband to join him for dinner. She was a teacher in a junior high school [now middle school] in San Francisco. I had no idea that Julia was in this area, since I had lost touch when I left Carthage High School and went to the University of Texas. She was a couple of grades behind me in Carthage High. As a small girl, she had visited in our home in Murvaul and played dolls with my sister, Lois. Her mother and Tex's mother were sisters. We were not related; however, she called my mother Aunt Daisy and I called her mom Aunt Mae. Julia's husband, Ed Ross, was from Marshall, Texas, and worked as an engineer-rodman for the Texas & Pacific Railroad before they moved to the West Coast. He was now teaching "quickie" math courses to servicemen in a trade school in San Francisco.

Tex also told us that he had asked Julia to bring "Frenchie" [Jeannette] along. She was a single woman of French background who was teaching French and English in another junior high school (Aptos) in San Francisco. She rented a room from the Rosses in their home [in San Francisco]. Since I had not seen Julia in over 20 years, Tex arranged our meeting in his usual dramatic fashion. When they arrived in the hotel lobby, we were not introduced. He had previously arranged for Forbess and me to follow Tex and his guests into the elevator. So, we entered the elevator with Tex, the Rosses and "Frenchie," who had come. On the way up, Tex tried his pidgin French on "Frenchie," which caused her to laugh. We left the elevator on the same floor as previously arranged and followed Tex and his guests into Tex's room. As we started to enter the room, Ed Ross stopped us with: "You must have the wrong room!" I replied: "Isn't this Tex's room?" Tex added: "Do I know you?" Julia stared at me intently. Tex just wanted to see if she would recognize me after twenty years. Then to my surprise, Julia blurted out: "Why, Rex Ritter, it is you, isn't it?" Then I asked how she recognized me after all those years. When I last saw her, I weighed only 125 pounds—now I weighed 165 pounds! She said she first thought I was Uncle Zack (that is what she always called my father), but she knew he would not be in a navy uniform—so it had to be me. Lieutenant Commander Forbess, the other Texan, and I were officially introduced to Ed Ross (Julia's husband) and

Jeannette Rouyet ("Frenchie"). We then went out to a reunion dinner for Julia and me. We had a nice dinner as Tex's guests, and Julia and Ross (that is what she always called him) invited me to visit their home in San Francisco. They had married in Longview while she was living with her uncle and family, Dr. Adams, after her mother's death. This was really a great reunion with Julia after all the years and having lost track of her completely.

During the next few weeks, I saw a lot of Jeannette, with both Julia and Tex in the role of matchmaker. One night I arrived late at Julia's house with Tex and his wife Dorothy Fay. Jeannette had already retired, but Julia insisted that she get up and greet the guests. It was early morning before we left. Then Jeannette drove me back to the base at Camp Parks. She returned home just in time to wash her face, have a cup of coffee and go to school. This was really rough on this little junior high school teacher, but she took it in stride and with grace.

During this period, I spent more time in San Francisco than at Camp Parks—however, my very capable executive officer, Howard McKay, covered for my absence. He said he was repaying me for the times I did the same for him at Camp Endicott when his wife would meet him in New York City. I spent many nights in San Francisco at the St. Francis, Fairmont or Sir Francis Drake in one of their dormitory rooms.

Jeannette had a little gray Chevrolet Coupe and a "B" gas ration card [which she saved after the war]. She would tease me by saying: "You were looking for a blonde with an 'A' ration card—but had to settle for a brunette with a 'B' card." She had a secret admirer who owned a filling station in San Jose near her parents' home, where she could get gas without using her scarce coupons. This was a very convenient arrangement for me to share her wheels as well as her pleasant company.

Jeannette did volunteer duty after school at the Pepsi-Cola Serviceman's [and Women's] Center on [948] Market [and Mason] St. in San Francisco.[3] Once, I met her there dressed in my favorite

3. The Pepsi-Cola Center for Servicemen opened in March 1943, which was mentioned in the "List of Events for Service People" in the *San Francisco Chronicle* (*SFC*) and the *San Francisco Furlough Guide* during the war. I still have a postcard of it, along with my grandmother's volunteer pin. Gladys Hansen, *San Francisco Almanac: Everything You Want to Know About The City* (San Rafael,

blue-gray uniform with the lieutenant commander shoulder boards. I must have seemed out of place there, since the center was primarily for enlisted personnel. When I approached the counter where she was working, she deflated me with: "Look who's here in all his trappings!" Later, she told me about the time a sailor approached the counter and inquired: "Where is the 'head'?" One of the teachers at the counter with her replied: "the 'head'? the head of what?" Then Jeannette spoke up and said: "It is down the hall to your right." Jeannette then turned to her companion and said: "He was looking for the restroom." Her friend asked her how she knew that. She replied: "I happen to be dating a sailor now!" The sailor turned out to be me, a lieutenant commander.

During all these pleasant dates with Jeannette, the war seemed far away. I tried to forget that on any day now, I would receive orders to move my battalion south to Port Hueneme for final outfitting prior to departing for overseas duty. Would this be the end of what I considered a beautiful [wartime] romance?[4]

Jeannette's father and mother lived on Alum Rock in East San Jose. Her brother, Adrian (1915–1984), was in the Army Air Force in Natal, Brazil. One evening I was invited to join her for dinner at her parents' home. I took a Greyhound bus to San Jose and got a room at the old Sainte Claire Hotel. Jeannette picked me up at the hotel and drove me to her parents' home. The house was nestled behind tall palm trees in a delightful setting, on a 10 acre fruit ranch.[5] Her father [Jean Baptiste Rouyet (c. 1885–1949)]

---

CA: Presidio Press, 1980), 53. Other USO places in San Francisco, such as the Stage Door Canteen near Union Square and Hospitality House at Civic Center (now the site of the Main Library) near City Hall, were also for enlisted military personnel before they shipped out to the Pacific from the naval bases in the Bay Area or the San Francisco Port of Embarkation (SFPE).

4. In the 1940s San Francisco was called the "City of Romance" in *San Francisco in the Forties* (also titled *San Francisco in the 1940s*) (1986) about San Francisco during World War II. It was part of a documentary series on the city's history from the Gold Rush to the late 20th century.

5. In the 1940s, the Santa Clara Valley was called "The Valley of Hearts' Delight," which was the name of a promotional silent film in the 1920s, before it became Silicon Valley, just before and during World War II. In 2009 History San Jose had an exhibit on wartime San Jose called *Home Front: Santa Clara Valley's Experience in World War II*.

was a retired French baker and was a sort of a gentleman farmer. Mr. Rouyet was a stocky fellow with a twinkle in his eye and a rare sense of humor. He reminded me of my own father, though they had dissimilar backgrounds. Both Mr. and Mrs. Rouyet were born in the South of France and came over here as adults [in 1902 and 1905, respectively]. They met and married over here [date unknown but probably c. 1906–1907], where he had learned the baker's trade. Jeannette's mother, Josephine, had a queenly appearance and a beautiful complexion, accented by beautiful gray hair.

We had cocktails before dinner, which I believe was sweet vermouth with a cherry. Just before dinner, her father tried on my navy coat-and blue-grey uniform with the shoulder boards—and strutted around proudly. We had a real gourmet dinner, prepared by her mother, who modestly explained to me that she thought of it as everyday fare. It was truly an enjoyable evening. Mr. Rouyet explained to me that he had retired at age 51 because he could not bear having the union tell him how to conduct his own business. This was quite a revelation to me. Here was a farm boy from a small village in the Lower Pyrenees, who had come here at age 17— could not speak the language—learned a trade and ran his bakery business (French Bread) for years—raised two fine children [in Sausalito, Alameda, and San Jose] and sent them through college. Who said this was not the land of opportunity? As Jeannette drove me back to the hotel, I felt sure I had been accepted by her parents, despite our differences in culture [and religion, since my grandfather was Methodist and my grandmother was Catholic]. I returned to Camp Parks with a warm feeling about meeting her parents.

Before leaving Camp Parks, I felt I should know the type of duty we might encounter in the war zone. This would help us to select both the equipment and the training we should have. I could find out nothing from the command at this base. Another OINC of a Seabee unit told me I should go see Capt. Cushing Phillips, Exec to Rear Admiral Carl Cotter, Director of the Pacific Bureau of Yards & Docks, whose office was on Market Street in San Francisco. He told me that my battalion would be going to Kwajalein after its recapture from the Japanese [scheduled for early 1944]. I had to keep this secret, but now I knew how to plan.

The next time I saw Jeannette was in San Francisco. After dinner we had a drink at the Patent Leather Bar on the mezzanine of the St. Francis Hotel.[6] I told her I had found out my destination in the war zone, but had to keep it secret. Now there was no doubt where we were going—but some doubt as to how long I would be overseas. I mentioned that I had met Rear Admiral Carl Cotter's Executive Officer and he had given me the word. Jeannette told me she knew Cotter's wife, Kay. She had been a teacher here and later in Hawaii.[7] She told me that the last time she saw Kay, she had borrowed 50 cents for carfare and had not repaid the debt. I told her that the admiral was my big boss—so just forget about the debt! Just before leaving this spot in the St. Francis, we agreed we expected to marry. However, we felt we were both mature enough to wait and see how we felt about marriage after my return from overseas. After reaching this conclusion I saw Jeannette home and then spent the night in the Fairmont officer's dorm.

On Friday morning, November 5, 1943, I returned to Camp Parks just in time to learn that we had orders to move the battalion to Camp Rousseau, Port Hueneme, on Tuesday, November 9. Although I had expected these orders, the word came as quite a shock. That afternoon, I tried to reach Jeannette in San Francisco by phone. She and Julia had already left for her parents' home in San Jose. I was disappointed in not being able to reach her before she left. Now I was not sure I would be able to see her again before we left to go south. Perhaps, I might be able to see her again on Sunday night if she returned from San Jose in time. I decided to call her at her parents' home in San Jose to arrange to see her before we left for Port Hueneme.

Later on Friday night, I managed to contact Jeannette by phone in San Jose. I told her of our imminent departure for Port Hueneme. I will never know why, but suddenly I blurted out: "Let's get married!" "When," she said, "if you think you can make it." Then she told me that she and Julia would return from San Jose, via Camp

---

6. The Patent Leather Bar (1939–1953) was a favorite drinking and meeting spot in San Francisco, along with the Top of the Mark and the Starlight Roof at the Sir Francis Drake in the 1940s. Herb Caen (1916–1997), the famous and legendary *San Francisco Chronicle* columnist for 58 years, called the St. Francis "the Frantic."

7. Kay sent my grandmother an airmail letter from Hawaii, which I still have, that was carried on the China Clipper on the return leg of its first round-trip flight from San Francisco to Manila, in November 1935.

Parks, on Saturday morning—and we would take it from there. I knew no waiting period to get married was required in California during wartime; however, the blood test was still required. Early on Saturday morning, I dropped into the dispensary at the base to see my old friend, Dr. Bernstein, whom I had known in the 8th Seabees in Dutch Harbor. He was on the staff of the base medical force. When I told him I needed a blood test to get married on Sunday, he called his chief hospital corpsman and told him to take care of me. The corpsman said: "Come on in, Commander, and we will start the test." Dr. Bernstein yelled out: "Hell, Chief, never mind the test, just give him the paper—can't you see he is in a hurry, since he is getting married tomorrow. He hasn't time to wait for any test results." The chief prepared the blood test paper and gave it to me, just in time for me to go to the main gate at the base to meet Jeannette and Julia. It was nice to have an old friend like Dr. Bernstein.

We drove to City Hall in San Francisco to get our marriage license. The clerk could not issue the license until Jeannette could produce her blood test. He agreed, however, to prepare the license and hold it pending our return with her blood test. He even agreed to take the license home with him where we could pick it up if we did not return before his office closed. In the meantime, we called her friend, Paul MacDonald, a jeweler in downtown San Francisco, for both an engagement ring and a wedding ring—one for me, too. This really had been a busy Saturday. Thanks to efforts of Julia and Jeannette, we would be able to get everything ready for our wedding tomorrow. They shopped for clothes while I went to the florist. The lab did not complete Jeannette's blood test until after the clerk's office closed. It was after dark when we got the certificate. The clerk lived in the same area as Julia. We went to his house, produced the paper, and picked up the marriage license. Now we were all set to get married the following day.

On Saturday night, November 6, we had drinks and supper with Julia and Ross to celebrate having accomplished everything in one short day. Before, I knew it, it was time to go to bed and get some sleep before the wedding tomorrow. I anticipated no trouble in finding a bed at a dorm in one of the large hotels downtown. However, I forgot how late it was—and it was also Saturday night. Both the Fairmont and the Sir Francis Drake were full.

The St. Francis assured me that they could take care of me and to just come on down. When I arrived, they told me someone had made a mistake. They had no space in their officers' dorm. I had visions of spending my last night as a bachelor in a chair in the lobby of the St. Francis [which was very common for service personnel in wartime San Francisco]. The clerk then told me they could offer me a bed in the Turkish Bath area. Since I was quite weary from this busy day, and it was getting late, I accepted the clerk's offer. I slept on a cot in one of the cooling off cubicles connected with the Turkish Bath facility. I fell asleep immediately; however I was awakened many times during the night, when they would bring some noisy drunk into the area and sober him up in a Turkish Bath. My last night before getting married was unforgettable. Despite the fitful night in the Turkish Bath cubicle, after a hot shower and a good breakfast, I was able to face the reality of getting married.[8]

When I arrived at the Ross home on Ulloa Street, Jeannette's parents were already there, having driven up from San Jose. In a little while, we left for the church. The ceremony was short and simple, and suddenly I was no longer a bachelor. Only the Rosses and the Rouyets were present for the wedding. We returned to Julia's for one of her famous fried chicken dinners. Later, I met Lou Bouret, Jeannette's first cousin. Also, several of Jeannette's friends dropped by to offer congratulations. All in all, it was a pleasant and beautiful day. We spent our wedding night at the Alexander Hamilton Hotel. It is a nice, small hotel, just out of the downtown area. Our honeymoon was quite short, since I had to return to Camp Parks early Monday morning to get my battalion ready for our move south on Tuesday. Jeannette had to return to Aptos Junior High to teach her classes. We met at the hotel and spent Monday night together. On Tuesday morning, Jeannette drove me back to Camp Parks, since we would be moving our battalion out that day. She took the day off from school. It was decided that she would take leave from school and join me in Ventura on the weekend. Here, we hoped to continue our honeymoon.

8. There is a good description of the St. Francis during the war in a booklet called *The Westin St. Francis: Celebrating a Century of History on Union Square* (San Francisco, CA: The Westin St. Francis, 2006).

## En Route to Port Hueneme

Early on Tuesday morning, November 9, 1943, the 107th Seabees boarded some ancient, dusty coaches and left Camp Parks. As our train travelled south, I had time to reflect on my interesting stay at Camp Parks. I had met Julia Ross after 20 years. I had met— and married—a lovely lady after only three weeks acquaintance— although I felt I had known her much longer due to the association with Julia Ross. I will always be grateful for Tex Ritter's telegram asking me to join him at the Leamington Hotel in Oakland—and for Julia bringing Jeannette over. After Jeannette returned to school and announced her leave to join me in Ventura, some of her teacher friends asked where she first met me. She told them the truth: "In a hotel bedroom in Oakland." Very true: however, she could have added: "You know there's a war on."

On Wednesday morning, November 10, we arrived at Port Hueneme, some 50 miles north of Los Angeles. This is the Seabee center for the West Coast, as Camp Endicott is for the East Coast. The base is two miles from Oxnard and about six miles from Ventura. This was the main outfitting and embarkation point for Seabee units headed for the Pacific sector. Incidentally, I was the only person in our battalion who knew that our next destination was the Kwajalein Atoll in the Central Pacific.

## Port Hueneme, California

When the 107th debarked from the train on November 10, 1943, we were assigned quarters at Camp Rousseau on this Seabee base. I reported to Capt. H.P. ("Pete") Needham, who briefed me on our final training program before shipping out to Island X (Kwajalein). We were located only 50 miles from Los Angeles, so our personnel anticipated interesting liberty in Hollywood. Since my new wife was driving from San Francisco to Ventura on Saturday, November 13, I hastened to complete plans for our program at Camp Rousseau. These plans included both training and liberty schedules. Our artisans were assigned to various shops located in large Quonsets to build mock-up structures simulating overseas facilities—and then dismantle them for others to repeat the training process. Military training schedules were also set up. Our supply department was very busy acquiring equipment and supplies to take with us when we left for our overseas base. We felt that we might be leaving here within two weeks, in view of the furious pace of our schedules. How wrong we were!

Late on Saturday afternoon, Jeannette arrived at Ventura in her little gray Chevrolet, which she dubbed "Matilda." Julia Ross came down with her. I arranged rooms for us at a small hotel near the railroad station. Jeannette had taken an indefinite leave of absence from the school district in San Francisco in order to be with me while I was stationed at Port Hueneme, about 15 miles south. Julia had to return to her school on Monday, so we put her aboard the "Daylight," the crack Southern Pacific train, for her return to San Francisco.

Since we did not care just to live in a hotel room during our stay together, we started looking for a motel with a kitchenette. Some of my officers' wives had arrived in advance of the battalion and had found space in a motel south of town. Jeannette inquired there but found no vacancies. However, she heard that there was a vacancy at the Rex Hotel (really a motel) at the southern edge of Ventura. In order to ensure getting these accommodations from a lady manager with a reputation of being "picky," Jeannette put on her best suit and wore a hat. She was given the unit immediately. Now we could set up housekeeping and enjoy our delayed honeymoon. The kitchen was so small that it was difficult to accommodate two people at the same time, but she was able to prepare the meals here. I did not know before, but Jeannette was an excellent cook. This navy base had a rule that the OINC of a battalion could stay ashore only every other night. However, I managed to go back to the Rex Hotel every night—thanks to a competent Exec, Lieutenant McKay, who covered for me in admirable fashion. He remembered I had done the same for him while we were at Camp Endicott, allowing him to meet and stay with his wife from "Philly" in New York. Mac's wife did not come out to the West Coast.

On a weekend shortly after we arrived, we went down to Van Nuys to visit Tex and Dorothy Fay Ritter. He did not know we were married, so he put on quite a show about it with comments like: "I knew I should have pulled in the reins before this thing got out of hand." However, both he and Dorothy Fay were obviously pleased. They had a sprawling ranch home on about two acres in Van Nuys, with a horse lot and stable for his movie horse "White Flash."

Jeannette drew the assignment of cooking our supper on Saturday night. She had some difficulties due to the absence of supplies in the kitchen, but she made out in fine fashion.

My new wife was not only a good teacher, but also a fine cook. How lucky can one get? After supper, a horse trainer who had worked with Tex's horse, "White Flash," dropped by to see Tex. He was on his way to deliver "Champion," Gene Autry's horse, back home. He showed us a trick he had taught "Champion." He placed a shovel under the horse's tail and shouted: "Give Champion." Sure enough, to our complete surprise, the horse let go with a couple of horse biscuits. I inquired as to the value of this training. The trainer said: "One night Gene Autrey was on the stage with the horse doing the usual bowing to the applause when Gene turned to the audience and said: "Now you have seen what 'Champion' can do—now let's see if I can do as well." At that precise moment, the horse dropped several biscuits on the stage. Gene was embarrassed, but the crowd roared. This was really something.

A couple of weeks after our visit with the Ritters in Van Nuys, they came up to our place in Ventura. After cocktails, I announced that we would sojourn to a nearby cafe for dinner. Tex looked at Jeannette and said: "Hell, honey, can't you cook?" He already knew she could, but he was enjoying teasing this new bride. Anyway, she accepted the challenge and cooked a delicious meal in this tiny motel kitchen. For dessert, she served some home canned cherries her mother had given us. Tex really went all out for the cherries and then remarked: "You know, Jeannette, these cherries ain't fitten for dogs, but they are just fine for Texans." We all enjoyed the evening very much, feeling that each time together would be the last time before I would leave for the Pacific Sector.

Later, we had Lt. Cmdr. Sam Hamill and his wife to dinner in our quarters. Sam was with me in the Aleutians, both at Adak and Amchitka, where the Japanese dropped a bomb in our vicinity. Before the war, Sam had been in textiles back East, so Keith Wheeler in his book, *The Pacific Is My Beat*, referred to Sam as a "diaper salesman from New Jersey." Jeannette fixed her now famous "French chicken." Sam really knocked himself out on her specialty. On leaving, he suggested a repeat performance, adding that next time he would bring the chicken. Next time, we all went to the Pierpont Inn and enjoyed the view of the Pacific and a fine dinner. We really enjoyed staying at the Rex Hotel, which was our real honeymoon.

Just when I thought we would be receiving orders to ship out, we received a set of orders, dated November 22, 1943, instructing us to report to the commanding officer of the Acorn Training Detachment for assignment to Acorn Unit 23, for duty, including overseas duty, and training prior to departure. I reported to the C.O., Capt. Gurney, a naval flight officer, at Camp Bedillion. This facility was next door to Camp Rousseau and adjacent to "Holly-by-the-Sea," a shabby resort village on the Pacific Ocean. The two camps were separated by a high chain-link fence with sentries guarding the only gate between the two camps. The Acorn Training Detachment was humorously called "splinter city," probably on account of the wooden barracks. There was no love lost between Captain Gurney, a line naval aviator and Captain Needham, a Civil Engineer Corps officer. Since I frequently had business to transact with Captain Needham, I found it politic to leave Camp Bedillion by the West Gate facing the Pacific and travel around the base to the main entrance to Camp Rousseau, rather than pass through the sentries at the gate separating the two areas. I found it strange that such enmity could develop between two "four-stripers," both career naval officers. A reserve spot lieutenant commander found this hard to comprehend—but I respected it—and acted accordingly.

It did not take Captain Gurney long to find out that the 107th Seabees had an excellent band. So each morning, our band would provide the music for colors and a wave platoon marched by— all under the watchful eyes of many—including Captain Gurney. Also, our talents in the maintenance area came to light—so we became an adopted "Public Works Department" for Captain Gurney's Base. The captain was also in charge of an Advance Base at Point Mugu (we called it "Mudgu" for obvious reasons—it was muddy there). Here we were called to install "Marston Mat" landing strips on the beach so the captain could land and take off in his Piper Club. Point Mugu was located about five miles down the coast from our camp.

All of this was good training for our battalion. However, we noted that several battalions that arrived at Port Hueneme after we came had long since left for the Pacific area. I began to wonder what this long stay here might be doing to the morale of our people. Personally, I was enjoying the stay, since it extended my honeymoon. The captain issued me a personal jeep so I was able to drive to the motel in Ventura each evening, this despite the station rule requiring me to stay aboard every other night. Only once did I remain overnight at "Splinter City." A torrential rain preventing me from driving. Often, Jeannette would drive down and pick me up.

Occasionally Jeannette and I would drive down in the evening to the officer's club at Camp Rousseau for cocktails and dinner. This was a nice officer's club. The food and atmosphere were great. We would also meet fellow CEC Officers in the battalion on this base. Also, we would visit Bard's Barn, another clubhouse on the base, for a party and a dance. This building had been Senator Bard's residence before the navy took over this area. We also made several trips to Santa Barbara.[9] Occasionally, we would have dinner at the Santa Barbara Biltmore Hotel, which was a famous resort overlooking the Pacific Ocean. Also, when we drove up to Santa Barbara, about 40 miles north of Ventura, we would go to the Montecito Country Club for their Saturday night buffet dinner. Later, we would see a current movie in the lounge of the club house. They always treated us nicely there and the atmosphere was very pleasant. As we drove up to the club house, we could see several of the fairways on the golf course. I often hoped that I could return some day and play this fine course—I did much later.

For Christmas 1943, Jeannette and I drove to San Jose to visit to her parents. En route, we stopped at a liquor store in Carpinteria [southeast of Santa Barbara] to purchase a bottle to take to her father. To my chagrin, Jeannette had to go in to make the purchase, since no one in uniform was allowed to buy liquor until after 1700—a rule that the services had made to curb the personnel drinking during the day. Later, we stopped at Andersen's Split Pea Inn, in Buellton, south of Santa Maria and west of Solvang, the colorful Danish community [which didn't acquire its distinctive Danish village architecture until after the war]. This inn is a favorite

9. There is a photo of my grandparents in front of Mission Santa Barbara in late 1943–early 1944.

tourist attraction—noted for its split pea soup. We planned to buy another bottle here. We were told that one must buy a bottle of wine or rum before buying the hard stuff. Jeannette walked up to the clerk and boldly asked for a bottle of Scotch. He seemed a bit flustered at her audacity. Anyway, we acquiesced and bought a bottle of wine—and then Scotch.

We arrived in San Jose after dark and had a nice visit with her folks. We also had a visit with Julia and Ross. Also, I got to meet some of Jeannette's relatives, including Uncle and Aunt Bouret, who had a vineyard on the outskirts of San Jose. They were Lou Bouret's parents. I had met Lou right after our wedding. The French have an interesting custom: they call their uncles and aunts by their last name. All this was just like being at their home for Christmas. It was great to see that Jeannette's parents completely accepted me as a member of the family. I felt I might be taking their son's place—home for Christmas—who was far away in Natal, Brazil. We reluctantly returned to Ventura and to my Duty Station at Port Hueneme.

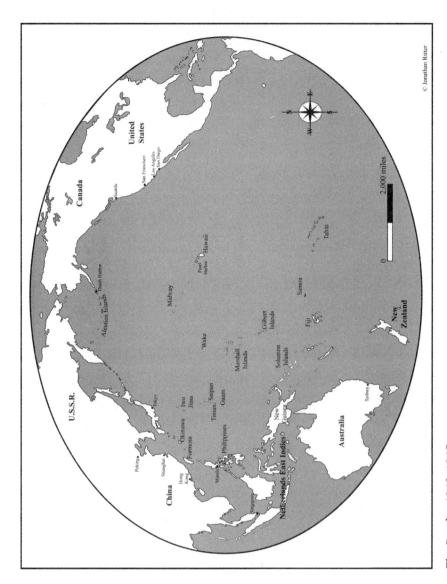

The Pacific, 1942–1945

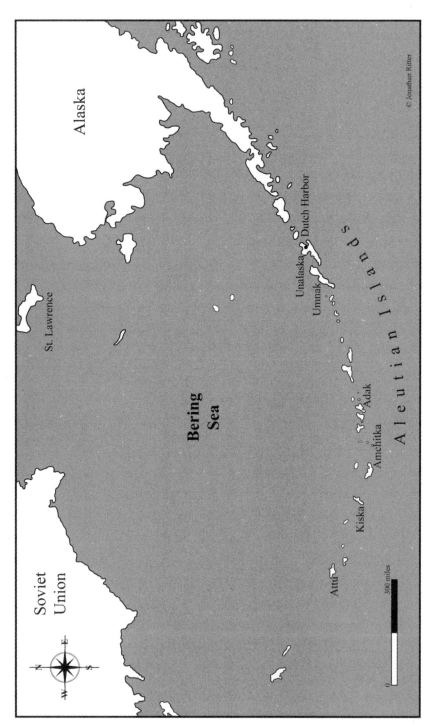

The Aleutians

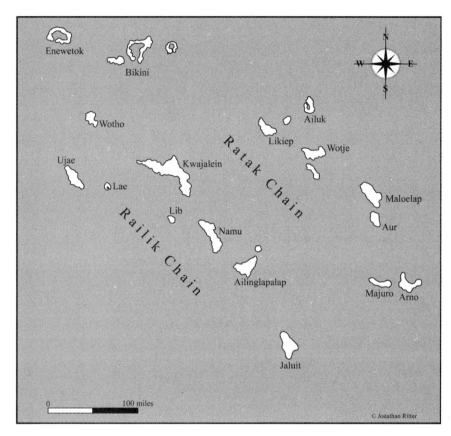

The Marshalls

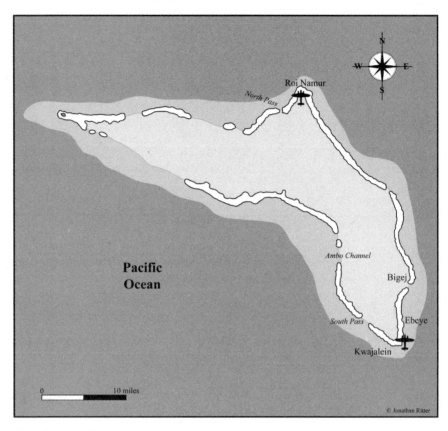

Kwajalein Atoll

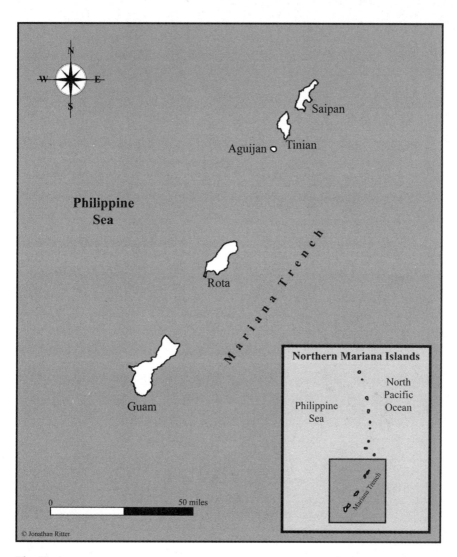

The Marianas

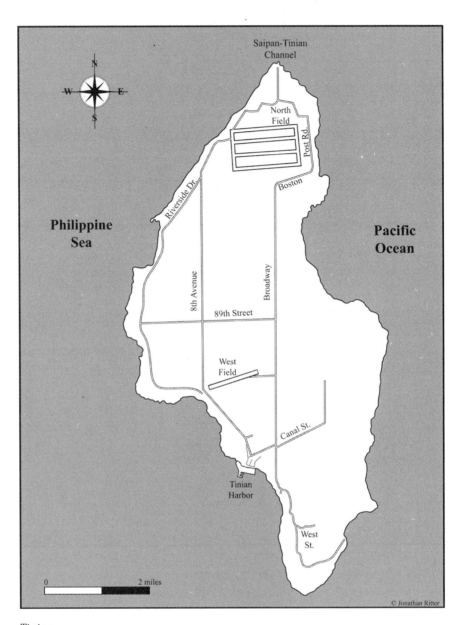

Tinian

Lt. Cmdr. J.R. Ritter (*seated front row, center*) and officers of the 107th Seabee Battalion at Camp Endicott, Davisville, RI, July 31, 1943. (Author Photo)

J.R. and Jeannette Ritter in Santa Barbara, CA, late 1943–early 1944. (Author Photo)

Painting of the 107th Seabees at work, Port Hueneme, CA, 1944, by M. Loew, Battalion Artist. (Author Photo)

So when we reach the "Isle of Japan" With our caps at a Jaunty tilt We'll enter the city of Tokyo On the roads the SEABEES Built.

Third Marine 2ND Raider R

Marine and Seabee with sign on Bougainville Island, British Solomon Islands, ca. 1943. (Courtesy of *Seabee* Magazine–US Navy Seabee Museum)

Seabee sign on Bougainville Island, British Solomon Islands, January 2, 1944. (Courtesy of *Seabee* Magazine–US Navy Seabee Museum)

Lt. Cmdr. J.R. Ritter (*middle row, second from left*) and officers of the 107th Seabee Battalion on Tinian, ca. 1945. (Author Photo)

The 107th Seabee Monument, Tinian. (Courtesy of Panoramio.com)

North Field, Tinian, 1945. (USAAF Photo)

B-29 in flight. (USAAF Photo)

Surrender of Japan, USS *Missouri*, Tokyo Bay, September 2, 1945. Photograph from the US Army Signal Corps Collection–U.S. National Archives. (Courtesy of the US Navy–Naval History and Heritage Command)

The Seabee Memorial, Arlington, VA. (Author Photo)

# Chapter 5

❖

❖

❖

❖

❖

# 1944: The Central Pacific: Kwajalein and Bigej

Early in 1944, Tex Ritter rounded up several of his Hollywood associates and put on a "free" show at the theater in "Splinter City," Camp Bedillion. This free show for all hands had lots of expensive talent from movies and Western music. Everyone seemed to enjoy the performance. This event really set me up with my battalion and the Acorn 23 personnel. I was grateful to Tex for this gesture. My immediate superior was Cmdr. "Bill" Hopf, a naval aviator and C.O. of Acorn 23, to which my battalion was attached. His exec was Lt. Cmdr. Heintz. This combination inspired my French wife to come up with: "What a combination to send to the war zone in American uniforms—Hopf, Heintz and Ritter."

On February 20, 1944, we received orders to load the 107th Construction Battalion and Acorn 23 aboard the *Sea Pike*, a navy transport, with our gear, supplies and equipment, for our initial destination of Pearl Harbor, [Oahu], Hawaii. In the meantime, I had persuaded Commander Hopf that it would be better if he and I flew to Pearl Harbor from San Francisco to make any necessary arrangements for the arrival of the *Sea Pike* with our troops. He agreed and had wheedled a rather vague set of orders for us to proceed ahead of our personnel. Our executive officers would be in charge on the navy transport. I was happy with this development. I could have a little more time with my wife—and avoid the dreary ride aboard the *Sea Pike*.

Late on February 20, Jeannette and I, with Commander Hopf, watched the final loading of personnel on the *Sea Pike* during a steady rain. Most of the wives who had been there with their husbands were on hand and followed the ship to the end of pier as it sailed out for Pearl Harbor. As the ship cleared the dock, they waved furiously to "Ritter's Critters," as they now called themselves. I did not envy them the trip during this season of the year.

Jeannette and I said goodbyes to our friends on both of the bases at Port Hueneme—and said goodbye to Port Hueneme for a while. We had stayed here over three months. It had been a glorious honeymoon that was now coming to an end. Later, we bade farewell to our little unit at the Rex Hotel in Ventura, and headed north in the little grey Chevrolet for San Jose and San Francisco.

## San Francisco

Commander Hopf and I had orders to report to COM SERV PAC at Pearl Harbor by Naval Air from San Francisco. En route from Port Hueneme and Ventura, Jeannette and I stopped by San Jose for a nice, farewell visit with her parents. Then we drove to San Francisco and went to Julia and Ross's house, while I awaited the first available air transportation to Pearl Harbor. Jeannette would now terminate her leave of absence from Aptos Junior High School. She would be teaching there again, pending my return from the Pacific Area. Shortly, I would be flying out to Pearl Harbor to rejoin my battalion.

On the evening of February 24, 1944, Jeannette and Julia drove me over to the Administration Building at Treasure Island Naval Station.[1] There I boarded a Pan Am China Clipper, under

1. The Administration Building or Building One, was the administration building for the 1939–1940 Golden Gate International Exposition (GGIE), which my grandmother visited. It was the headquarters of Treasure Island Naval Station from 1941 until the station closed in 1997. It was also the home of the original Treasure Island Museum from 1975–1997. A new museum on Treasure Island's history has been in the works since 2010. *See* Lt. Comdr. E.A. McDevitt, USNR, ed. *The Naval History of Treasure Island* (San Francisco: U.S. Naval Training and Distribution Center, 1946); http://tima.mobi/statues/lobbygallery

charter to the navy. This plane was one of the original fleet of passenger sea planes that flew the Pacific Area before the Pearl Harbor attack.[2] After boarding there was a delay in the takeoff, so I went back ashore. Jeannette and Julia were still waiting, so I had a brief, final visit. After a few minutes, I returned to our China Clipper. We taxied onto San Francisco Bay and made our takeoff from the water. As our plane roared over the Golden Gate Bridge, I could see the warning lights on top of the bridge. I could not help but wonder how long it would be before I would see them again and rejoin my lovely wife. We were served a steak dinner and later went to bed in bunks provided. What a convenience to be able to stretch out to sleep while en route to Pearl Harbor. I mused to myself: "This is the only way to fly." It would take us all night to reach our destination—Pearl Harbor [18 hours].

## *Pearl Harbor*

I awoke early on the morning of February 25, 1944. Our Clipper had already landed in the bay at Pearl Harbor and was taxiing into the seaplane dock. Commander Hopf and I debarked from the plane and went to breakfast in a Navy Officer's Mess at the Naval Station, Pearl Harbor [now Joint Base Pearl Harbor-Hickham].

We were not quite sure just how we should go about reporting in to some command. Our orders issued by Captain Gurney at Port Hueneme were quite vague. I suggested that we delay reporting to anyone until we had had a chance to case the place first to get the lay of the land. (My tour in the Aleutians had taught me this.) Since Captain Hopf was a naval aviator, he elected to go over to Naval Air Station Ford Island, in Pearl Harbor.[3] I decided to drop in at CINCPAC, Admiral Nimitz's Command, on the navy base [from 1941–1945]. I knew that Neil Kingsley, former Exec and OINC of the 4th Seabees up in Dutch Harbor, was here on the CINCPAC staff, and I felt that I could depend on my old friend,

2. Before 1939, the Clippers flew from Alameda. During the Fair on Treasure Island, they were berthed in the cove between the island and Yerba Buena Island. The Clipper base moved from Treasure Island to Mills Field (SFO) in 1945.

3. The wreck of the USS *Arizona*, which was destroyed in the Pearl Harbor attack, lies just off Ford Island and has been covered by the Memorial since 1962. In 1943, the *Arizona*'s superstructure was removed along with 400 bodies. The bodies of 700 officers and men still remain on the ship. (https://www.nps.gov/valr/index.htm)

Neil, to "give me the real scoop." It was good to see Neil again. As a former Naval Academy man and a full-fledged commander in the CEC, he held an important position on the staff of Admiral Nimitz. He told me that the OINC of the Seabee Brigade here was expecting the 107th Seabees to arrive shortly and had specific plans regarding my battalion.

I was glad that I came to see my old friend, Neil Kingsley, at CINCPAC Headquarters. He told me that the Construction Brigade Commander planned to intercept the 107th Seabees on their arrival and replace them with another battalion that had been training at Red Hill, near Pearl Harbor. My battalion would be stationed at Red Hill for further training prior to being assigned another duty in the war zone. This other battalion would then board the transport with Acorn 23 to proceed to Kwajalein Atoll. Neil also told me that most of the "so-called" training at Red Hill was Quonset hut erection to house other Seabee units expected at Pearl. The idea of inflicting more unnecessary training on the 107th did not appeal to me. I felt that my battalion had had enough training and was ready to go into the war zone.

Later, I met Commander Hopf and reported my findings at CINCPAC. I told him that if he would like to dump the 107th and pick up a more seasoned battalion for Acorn 23, this was his chance. We could report in to CINCPAC and await the arrival of the *Sea Pike*. He insisted that he wanted to keep me and my battalion with his Acorn Unit. He also said he had found out that we could report with our basic orders to the Naval Air Station at Ford Island. I was pleased that Commander Hopf wanted to keep the 107th—and also happy that Neil Kingsley had provided me with the warning in time to save us.

We reported to the C.O. at Ford Island, across the Bay from CINCPAC, and were assigned quarters in the BOQ there. CINCPAC seemed far away now and we gave that command a wide berth. The quarters and food were fine at Ford Island, so we just rested and kept a low profile while we anxiously awaited the arrival of the *Sea Pike* with our troops from Port Hueneme.

Our troop transport arrived on February 26, 1944, and fortunately docked at Iroquois Point, across the Bay from Honolulu and CINCPAC. Commander Hopf and I met the transport and went aboard to see our execs and greet our troops. We allowed a few select officers and chiefs to go over to Honolulu on liberty, with instructions not to identify their units. We were fearful that if our presence was detected the 107th would be lifted and sent up to Red Hill. Two days later, we were on hand to see all our people reloaded on the *Sea Pike* and sailing for Kwajalein Atoll. My battalion had "escaped the net" the brigade had for us. In the meantime, Commander Hopf had already arranged for the two of us to fly out by navy air and meet our troops on their arrival in Kwajalein. It was with a sigh of relief that I saw the 107th sailing out of Pearl Harbor, in lieu of being detained here for an indefinite period.

On February 29, 1944, I received orders from Commander, Naval Air Force, Pacific Fleet to report to C.O. Acorn 23 (Commander Hopf) for duty as OINC of the 107th Construction Battalion—and to the Commandant, 14th Naval District, for first available air transportation to join our troops in Kwajalein. Commander Hopf had already been doing his homework to insure our continued association with his Acorn Unit. Now, we would be able to fly out and meet our people in Kwajalein.

## Tarawa, Gilbert Islands [three months after the 1943 battle]

On March 1, 1944, Commander Hopf and I boarded a naval air transport plane headed for a destination in the Gilbert Islands [now the Kiribati Islands]. We could not go directly to Kwajalein as planned, since it had not yet been taken from the Japanese. En route to Tarawa, we touched down for refueling at Johnson Island. This island is barely long enough for a short landing strip and is very narrow. How our navy pilot found this tiny spot in the middle of the Pacific Ocean, I will never know. Later, we landed at Tarawa. Everywhere we noted evidence of the terrific battle that had ensured the dislodging of the Japanese from this small island [less than one square mile]. Wrecked U.S. landing craft on the coral reef at the shore line gave mute evidence to the losses our marines had sustained making a beachhead.[4]

---

4. In the Battle of Tarawa (Operation Galvanic), the Seabees had been sent in during the first wave on November 20, 1943—D-Day, and had suffered heavy losses, which led to a change in future tactics, when the Seabees would only be sent in after an island was relatively secure.

We spent several days on this littered spot in the Gilbert Islands. The airstrip was barely usable after being repaired from the damage during the assault (which is why the island needed to be captured, because it had been a Japanese air base). It made one sad to surmise the number of U.S. Marines that lost their lives [about 991–1,000] capturing this desolate spot from the Japanese.[5] Perhaps, we should have pulverized it by air before the landing assault. All the personnel were literally camping out, pending facilities being built to support this airstrip. I was glad our units had not had to come here. Around March 4, 1944, our plane was able to leave Tarawa and fly to Kwajalein.

## Kwajalein, Marshall Islands

The airstrip on Kwajalein Island, at the south end of the atoll, had been secured from the Japanese [in Operations Flintlock and Catchpole, which were part of the Gilbert and Marshall Islands campaign from November 1943 to February 1944] and sufficiently repaired to permit our plane to land. We had a really rough landing on this recently repaired strip. Evidence of the terrible destruction inflicted by our naval forces and army landing units was visible on all sides. This place, like Tarawa, was really a mess. After landing, we were taken by a small boat to a yacht anchored in the lagoon, near Kwajalein Island, just inside the atoll. This yacht had been taken by the navy from Mr. McCormick, who had used it for Caribbean cruises before the war. The yacht was comfortable and made a fine floating BOQ. It was comfortable and the food was fine. This yacht was used for transient officers, like Commander Hopf and me. Here we were able to relax and await the arrival of the *Sea Pike* with our troops.

Kwajalein Atoll is the largest atoll in the world. It is over 60 miles long and 18 miles wide, surrounded by small islands, with small openings leading out to the Pacific. All the navies of the world could be anchored here in a safe harbor from the adjacent ocean. This ring of coral islands encloses this huge lagoon. Only a few channels were navigable from the ocean. From our vantage point on the yacht, we could see the next island

5. Japanese casualties in the Battle of Tarawa are still unknown. Out of 20,000 Japanese troops on Tarawa, only 17 surrendered. See "Pacific: February 1942–July 1945," *The World at War*, 1974.

away from Kwajalein on the east ring of the atoll. This island was called Ebeye and would be our own little Island X, our ultimate destination. Our air and sea units had done a complete job of destroying Ebeye. The place looked like a desert wasteland. Only bare trunks of palm trees stood silhouetted against the adjacent Pacific Ocean.

Although we had been told that some U.S. Army units had gone ashore on Ebeye, we were not all that sure the place was "secure." Commander Hopf and I decided to await the arrival of the *Sea Pike* with our troops before going ashore. It was quite possible that Japanese survivors could still be around in pillboxes that were visible in the field glasses from our yacht. Neither of us wished to be heroes at this stage of the game.

On March 7, 1944, the *Sea Pike* arrived and anchored in the lagoon a short distance from Ebeye Island. Commander Hopf and I left our comfortable home aboard the yacht and joined our people aboard the transport the next morning. Early on March 9, the small marine detachment aboard the *Sea Pike* was ordered to go ashore to scout the island to determine if it was safe to land our Seabees. Their young captain asked, "Why us, rather than the Seabees?" I said: "Because you are expendable—the Seabees are not!"

The captain took his detail ashore. In a short while the message came back to the ship that all was secure on Ebeye Island and it was safe to disembark our people. I sent an advance contingent of the 107th Seabees to set up a temporary camp and set up our mobile evaporators to provide freshwater. In a few days, all the 107th Seabees and Acorn 23 personnel were unloaded from the *Sea Pike*, together with all our supplies and equipment. Now, we were on our first Island X to start our first real job in the war zone. This is so much better than being detained for an indefinite period in Pearl Harbor in another training episode. We had come a long way since activation in Camp Peary on July 13, 1943—almost seven months. Since then we had passed through Camp Endicott, Camp Parks, Port Hueneme—and escaped the net at Pearl Harbor. My battalion was now ready to undertake our first mission in the [Central Pacific] war zone. I could feel that all hands were looking forward to getting the show on the road.

## *Ebeye Island, Marshall Islands*

The 107th Seabees and Acorn 23 landed on Ebeye Island on March 9, 1944. This island is a long, flat, narrow sand strip on the southeast corner of the Kwajalein Atoll. It is separated from the main island of Kwajalein by a narrow, rocky shoal which is almost inaccessible by land vehicles, even during low tide. This coral strip that was to be our home for a while is 4500 feet long and about 500 feet wide and only about four feet above high tide. A tropical storm could probably send waves crashing over the surface of the island.

Our fleet and air units had done a more complete job than the earlier one at Tarawa. The place was barren and a scene of utter destruction. Our ships and bombers had really wreaked vengeance here. Dead Japanese were still scattered around. Many were still in their fortified pillboxes, with their heads blown off. They had obviously held live hand grenades to their chests and had blown off their heads, rather than face surrender. Such dedication to the Emperor! We marveled at their dedication on this miserable island, so far from their homeland. Carrion birds were still feasting on the corpses, and the stench was awful.[6]

After we landed our people on the island, our first job was to bury the dead Japanese. The earlier army units that had visited Ebeye had done little cleanup. At least they had determined that the island was safe for us to come ashore. We used our bulldozers to make a common grave and push the rotting bodies into this trench and then fill in to cover the corpses. Now we were ready to start our mission on the island.

The basic mission for my Seabees on Ebeye was to restore the seaplane base the Japanese had operated here and to build facilities for Acorn 23 to operate a seaplane base for our navy. The Japanese seaplane facilities were completely destroyed—so we could start from scratch. Even the seaplane ramp extending out into the lagoon had been severely damaged by our bombing attacks. A concrete pier for docking small craft with shallow drafts was still intact.

Originally we set up tent camp facilities. We had plenty of fresh water, though it was rationed, due to the efforts of my men who

6. Which along with combat is what veterans, especially ground troops, mostly remember about any war.

ran the distillation unit to convert salt water from the lagoon to fresh water. Then we started Quonset hut erection for quarters, messing, administration, and hospital. The 107th continued to live in tents, since our stay was temporary—we would leave for another job after completion of a nose hanger for the repair of seaplanes. We found a damaged Japanese large concrete mixer and set up a central concrete plant for constructing foundations and repairing the damaged seaplane ramp. We even used captured Japanese cement left on the island—but found it was inferior to ours. While digging trenches for water and sewage systems with a backhoe, we seemed to invariably uncover dead Japanese we had originally buried. This caused some wit in the battalion with a morbid sense of humor to comment: "There seems to be a 'Nip' [Japanese] in the air this morning."[7]

The 107th made splendid progress on the construction of the facilities to permit Acorn 23 to operate a seaplane base here—as the Japanese had done when they controlled this island. We lived in a tent city on the north end of the island. The permanent facilities for the seaplane base were under construction in the central and south part of the island. The base hospital was constructed with a unique design, originated by our engineers in Headquarters Company. This involved wood frame vertical walls topped with a standard Quonset. In this way, we developed two story wards, thereby doubling the floor space under the same roof. Our distillation units were running 24 hours a day to provide a supply of fresh water to meet the ever-increasing demand. I was pleased with the speed demonstrated by our Seabees in completing facilities for the base. Commander Hopf, the skipper of Acorn 23, complimented us for the magic we were performing in transforming a wasteland into an operating facility. Our people also enjoyed seeing the construction progress—after all, we were doing what we had been trained to do.

Providing facilities for the operation of seaplanes from Ebeye won immediate results. Navy seaplanes were leaving this base each

7. During the Pacific War, most of the service personnel in the Pacific and Americans at home referred to the Japanese in racial and racist terms, as "Japs" and "Nips." There was even a 1944 Warner Brothers' *Looney Tunes* cartoon called "Bugs Bunny Nips the Nips." To his great credit, my grandfather generally used the more respectful term "Japanese."

day on various missions. Some involved enemy targets in places like Eniwetok, several hundred miles west, where the Japanese were still entrenched. The nose hanger our people had designed and built from a section of a large Quonset was used daily to service and repair returning seaplanes.

For several weeks after we arrived on the island, work progressed without interruption or interference either from within or without. Then it happened! Early one morning sirens on Kwajalein alerted us of an imminent air raid. We hit our foxholes as Japanese seaplanes passed over Ebeye Island dropping strings of anti-personnel bombs. Fortunately, no one was hurt by this raid, but we were just a bit wary now. Our camp was located adjacent to the fuel dumps at the north end of the island. Most of us accepted the raid as just a part of being in the war zone. I had previously experienced air raids in Amchitka (in the Aleutians), but this was the first for everyone else. Normally, the first air raid would not have been of great concern except for its effect on one of our officers, Lieutenant Cox. He was the C.O. of our headquarters company. After the raid, he spent most of his time near his foxhole. I was fearful that this example by one of our senior officers might adversely affect the morale of the men in his company—so in the meantime, I turned over his main duties to his assistant, Lt. (j.g.) Bliss Oliver. Incidentally, we had left Mr. Cox at Pearl Harbor with appendicitis when we came through. While recuperating, he spent some time with DIPRACDOCK at Pearl and tried to get a transfer to remain there. Obviously, he was just plain scared to be out here in the war zone. Otherwise, he was a fine gentleman and an excellent electrical engineer. Headquarters Company got along fine under Bliss Oliver.

A few days after the raid by the Japanese seaplanes, we heard our first—but not last—radio message from "Tokyo Rose." She was an American-born Japanese [Nisei] and defected to Japan after Pearl Harbor. [There were several "Tokyo Roses" during the war.] She broadcast in English to try and undermine the morale of U.S. personnel. That day she came on the radio with this stern warning: "You 107th Seabees had better evacuate the Marshall Islands if you want to see your loved ones again." Most of us were amused by her warning but really enjoyed the musical part of her program. This was better than the music we received over the American radio.

Later we had a ranking visitor who came over in a small boat from Kwajalein Island. He came over expressly to see me. He was RADM Carl Cotter, Director of the Pacific Bureau of Yards & Docks (DIRPACDOCK). He had flown in from Pearl Harbor. The staff of Acorn 23 and my own officers were visibly impressed by my distinguished visitor. He was in charge of all construction battalions in the Pacific [Theater]. He had just returned from San Francisco and brought me current news from my wife, Jeannette. His wife, Kay, had taught school with Jeannette, and they saw each other occasionally. Jeannette never met Admiral Cotter—nor had I ever met his wife, Kay. The late word he brought me from Jeannette came through his wife. This is the first time I had met him, though I had visited his San Francisco office and knew his exec, Capt. Cushing Phillips. It seems that Lieutenant Cox, who had been camping near his foxhole since the Japanese raid, had impressed the admiral's office in Pearl Harbor with his talent as an electrical engineer while recuperating from his appendicitis operation. Admiral Cotter said he would like to take him back to Pearl—if I could spare him. He offered to send me a replacement if I would release Lieutenant Cox to his office in Pearl. I told the admiral that Mr. Cox's assistant was quite capable of replacing him and taking over the duties of commander of our headquarters company. I told him no replacement would be needed. He was visibly pleased with my concurrence and made immediate arrangements for Lieutenant Cox to return to Pearl. I never told the admiral that he was doing us a favor to take him off our hands, since he was just plain scared out here in the war zone. I was very happy to meet this genial senior officer—my immediate superior.

The Acorn 23 Skipper, Commander Hopf, was a naval aviator and still drew flight pay. For some time, he had been unable to do any flying and was in danger of losing his flight pay. The army on Kwajalein had new light Piper Cubs used for reconnaissance around the atoll. Commander Hopf arranged to take one of these planes on a short flight in the area. He previously had flown in much heavier aircraft, such as carrier planes. He asked me to accompany him in the Piper Cub. I accepted with marked reluctance and on condition that he would make several passes low over the seaplane ramp on Ebeye, so I might inspect its condition. We had been making repairs on this damaged ramp. We took off from the strip on

Kwajalein without incident. This was a very small plane, and my knees were practically under his ears. He provided me with an excellent view of the seaplane ramp, which I would see quite well through the clear water. We also had a good view of other islands on the east side of the atoll, north of Ebeye. When we returned to the landing strip on Kwajalein, I could see he was having difficulty landing this light plane. Each time we touched the runway, a gust of wind would bear us aloft. He was obviously worried—and so was I. This would really be an untimely way to end our navy careers. Finally Bill (Commander Hopf) said: "Rex, we may have to run out of fuel before I can get this kite down." After four passes at the runway, he finally managed to keep the plane on the strip. We both breathed a sigh of relief as we got out of the Piper Cub. I suggested that he leave me back at the base the next time he wanted to get in his flight time.

We had no more Japanese air raids and our construction program proceeded ahead of schedule. Now we even found time for some recreation. We organized an officers' softball team and played army and marine units from the adjoining islands. I played left field, my old position in high school. Our first baseman was Lt. Cmdr. Bill Burkhard, a medical officer with Acorn 23. He was from San Francisco. We became fast friends—so when I returned to San Francisco after the war, he became my personal physician until his retirement.

Each morning around 0600, I would take a swim in the lagoon off the seaplane ramp. I usually went alone—which isn't such a good idea. One morning I took my usual swim and went out further in the lagoon than usual. I started to swim back to the seaplane ramp, but noted by sighting toward the barge pier that I was losing ground. The tide was taking me out into the lagoon away from the shore. There was no one in sight to rescue me, and I started to panic. Then I remembered my earlier Red Cross training while I was at the University of Texas at Austin. I quit fighting the tide, floated on my back, and calmly figured how I could reach the shore. I found that I could tack with the tide toward the North End of Ebeye Island. An hour later, I reached the shore—exhausted. This was really a close call. I never went out again.

Commander Hopf went back to Pearl Harbor for a conference. While he was away Lieutenant Commander Heintz was in charge of

Acorn 23. One morning he called me into his office and announced that henceforth he would hold mast on any of my Seabees who were up for disciplinary action. When I disagreed, he said there was no need to hold two separate masts, and he would do the job for both of us. I told him I would rather be responsible for discipline on my boys. He expressed concern, but dismissed by saying that was an order. I returned to my desk and remembered a letter from Frank Knox (1874–1944), Secretary of the Navy, stating that OINC's of construction battalions had the exclusive right to hold mast and dispense punishment to their men. I found a copy of this letter, and marched back to Heintz's office. When I showed this to him, he shouted at me: "Why wasn't I told about this order from Secretary Knox before?" "Sir," I said, "I had nothing to do with your indoctrination as a naval officer." He rescinded his previous order and told me to continue holding masts. I was relieved—I could think of nothing worse than having the commander of Acorn 23 discipline my men. He never mentioned the incident to Commander Hopf on his return. Neither did I.

Early in May 1944, I received my regular promotion to lieutenant-commander. I no longer held a spot promotion to that rank. I had been told earlier in Washington that when this happened, I would be spot promoted to commander. Nothing happened, despite the fact that BUDOCKS wanted all OINC'S of Seabee battalions to have the rank of commander. Later, I wrote to headquarters about my spot promotion to commander. I never received a reply—so I just contented myself to remain a lieutenant-commander for the duration.

We were fast completing our assignment at the seaplane base here. So, early in May, we detached Company D under Lieutenant McGill and a part of Headquarters Company to Bigej Island, about 20 miles north of Ebeye on the east coast of the atoll. Here, our mission was to build a fleet fuel farm and a fleet recreation center. On completion of our mission at Ebeye, the remainder of the battalion would join Co. D at Bigej, which had the secret code name of "Bennett."

On May 14, 1944, the Naval Air Base Ebeye was officially commissioned. A line officer came aboard and brought his flag there. Commander Hopf became commanding officer of the base, under the admiral. At the commissioning ceremonies, both the admiral and Commander Hopf lauded the 107th Seabees for a job well done. They both repeated the phrase, which has become the motto of the Seabees: "Seabees do the difficult jobs right away—the impossible ones take longer." In my brief remarks, I closed with: "This has been a practice run for the 107th—now we are ready." This had been quite an experience for us. I was justly proud of my unit.

Late in May, I flew to Enewetok for a visit to check progress on the air base there. This island had been recently captured from the Japanese [in February 1944]. My survey here indicated there appeared no reason for the 107th to move here, since normal progress in setting up the naval air base was sufficient. Our fleet and air units had not destroyed too much of the enemy installations. I spent a few pleasant days in Enewetok, visiting and swimming. Incidentally, I saw "Squeaky" Anderson here. The last time I saw him was in Adak in the Aleutians [in 1943]. He had participated in the marine assault on the island. I was surprised that the navy had let "Squeaky" leave the Aleutians. Next to the Japanese, he knew the area best. In fact, it was rumored he was engaged in smuggling activities in Alaska before the war. I returned to Ebeye to authorize the move of the rest of my battalion to Bigej, since we would not be needed there.

On May 26, 1944, we completed the move of the 107th from Ebeye to Bigej, where I reported to the army general at Kwajalein, as island commander of Bigej. We were detached from Acorn 23. Now, I had a command with a small contingent of marines under me to provide security. This would be an interesting experience being "on our own," with the army command miles away.

## Bigej Island, Marshall Islands

This island was entirely different from Ebeye. There had been little damage done here from our shelling. Vegetation and coconut trees were lush throughout the island. Also, we were on our own here, with little or no interference from the outside. The work of erecting fuel storage tanks and connecting pipelines proceeded rapidly. So did the job of constructing facilities for a fleet recreation area. We built playing fields, ball parks, bleachers, and a large Quonset as a basketball gym. It was intended that fleet personnel in the area would come here for R&R (Rest & Recreation), after we had completed our job and moved on. Also, the fleet would refuel from the storage tanks provided and a subterranean line out into the lagoon to the fleet anchor buoy. We enjoyed being on our own here. Our people used the recreational facilities off duty. The title of "Island Commander" enhanced my prestige—and age (41). Unfortunately, we had to cut down a few lovely coconut trees. At the top of each tree was a "cabbage," which we used to make "hearts of palm" salad. One night we were served a complete native dinner, including: breadfruit, heart of palm salad and fresh coconut. We were living on the land.

A short while after our whole battalion was settled on Bigej, I was faced with an unpleasant task. Before leaving Ebeye, I had a young seaman at mast charged with stealing a watch from a tent mate. Since he returned the watch, I gave him a warning, which was placed in his service jacket for 90 days. If he had no other offense within 90 days, the warning slip would be removed from his service record, giving him a clean bill of health with the navy. Incidentally, this warning system was initiated by me. Several career officers in the navy frowned on this technique, holding that any offense by an enlisted man should be part of his permanent record. However, I noted that later most of the OINC'S of the Seabee battalions adopted my warning system. During the 90-day period the warning slip was in a man's service jacket, he would not be eligible for promotion. The system worked very well in our battalion. I explained to the seaman that this was a sort of suspended sentence, and if another offense was committed during the 90-day period, the penalty of the first offense would be added to the second. I also told the seaman that stealing in any form could not be tolerated with six men occupying the same tent—and that any further similar act would result in a summary court martial.

One day, a marine sergeant brought the same man to me with the charge that he had stolen a rifle and some ammunition from the marine detachment on Bigej. I ordered a summary court (three officers from their battalion) to hear his case. They found him guilty. There were no mitigating circumstances, since there was no plausible reason for this theft. If he had needed a gun, it would have been issued to him. With much deliberation and with great reluctance, I gave him a BCD (Bad Conduct Discharge). This was the first serious disciplinary problem I had to deal with—and

I prayed it would be the last. He was sent back to his home in the States. Later I heard he had been drafted into the army and sent to the Central Pacific (General MacArthur's Theater). We never saw him again.

A little later, another unpleasant incident occurred. This involved our battalion chaplain, Father Fonash, a Catholic chaplain who had been assigned to the 107th while we were at Davisville, RI. He had enjoyed pleasant and easy duties at Newport involving officer cadets. It was obvious to me from the beginning that he was not happy with assignment to a Seabee battalion. Also, he appeared unsuited or unwilling to deal with the construction men that made up the bulk of our battalion. While we were at Port Hueneme, I contacted the district chaplain, a captain on the staff of the commandant, 11th Naval District at San Diego, suggesting a replacement. He would not even consider my request without my stating in writing that I considered him unfit to be a naval officer. I told the district chaplain that I could not in good conscience say that he was unfit—just that he was not temperamentally suited to deal with the Seabees in the war zone. Needless to say, I got nowhere with the district chaplain, so Father Fonash came along with the battalion to Kwajalein Atoll. He never really tried to be chaplain for the whole battalion—only for a few favorites. After we moved up to Bigej, he refused to live with the other officers and set up his quarters in his little tent chapel.

One day a young sailor of Greek background came to see me about emergency leave to go back to his home in San Francisco, since he had had word that his mother was ill and wished to see him. I checked and found out that that he had four older brothers at home, so that his presence was not really required to justify granting emergency leave. He persisted that he should be allowed to go home to see his mother, so I sent him over to talk it over with our chaplain. Subsequently, the chaplain and the Red Cross director on Kwajalein conspired to have a letter sent from Red Cross headquarters in San Francisco, stating that that the boy's presence was necessary. Normally, we abided by Red Cross findings, but I was convinced that this was a phony. I called the chaplain and the man to my office and told them bluntly that the circumstances did not warrant emergency leave, by navy standards—and I was forced to deny it—despite the Red Cross action. Now, I was firmly convinced that the battalion had to find a way to rid ourselves of this incompetent chaplain. This presented a problem—dumping a commissioned officer (chaplain) from the unit.

Late in May 1944, General Tenney, the atoll commander (my boss) sent me to Roi-Namur at the extreme north end of the atoll. There had been a few light Japanese air raids on installations there. He asked me to inspect the facilities to determine if there was sufficient damage to warrant sending a detail from the 107th to make repairs. I found no serious damage that would affect the ability of this facility to continue to carry out its assigned mission. I returned by the motor launch that had taken me to Roi-Namur and went to Kwajalein to report to General Tenney. He accepted my findings, so we did not have to send any of our people up to Roi-Namur. I enjoyed seeing more of this interesting atoll and was glad the general sent me up there.

A short time later I received secret orders to get the 107th Battalion in a state of readiness to move to Tinian Island in the Marianas, pending American forces taking this island from the enemy. On June 24, 1944,[8] I received orders to proceed to Pearl Harbor[9] on the first available Naval Air, in connection with our intended move to Tinian. Next day I left Ebeye Island on one of our seaplanes. It felt good to be able to utilize aircraft using the facility that my battalion had just completed.

## *Pearl Harbor*

On arrival at Pearl, I first went over to CINCPAC Headquarters to see if my old friend Cmdr. Neil Kingsley was still there. We had a nice reunion, and then I inquired from him how to go about

8. One month later the Battle of Tinian (July 24–August 1, 1944) began. It was covered in a recent article in the *WWII Quarterly* Winter 2019 issue titled "Taking Tinian."

9. This was a month after the explosion in West Loch on May 21, which killed 163 servicemen, which became 164 when a U.S. Navy diver died on one of the sunken LST's in West Loch in early 1945. This almost delayed Operation Forager, the invasion of Saipan, on June 15, which was largely overlooked because of D-Day (Operation Overlord) in Normandy on June 6. The disaster only caused one day of delay and one missing ship in the invasion. The West Loch disaster was classified until 1960 (https://www.stripes.com/news/2nd-pearl-harbor-kept-top-secret-until-1962-commemorated-1.410773)

changing chaplains—since I did not wish to take Fr. Fonash out
to Tinian. He sent me to the fleet chaplain on Admiral Nimitz's
staff. This fleet chaplain was a captain—and a Catholic. I feared
I might encounter the same problem I had earlier with the district
chaplain in San Diego. When I told the fleet chaplain about the
problem with our present chaplain and the recent episode in the
emergency leave case, he said I should not have to put up with
this in the war zone. I told him I agreed, but what could I do about
it? He told me he would find a more suitable chaplain to replace
Fr. Fonash. He must have sensed that I was not Catholic, so he said
that he presumed I would prefer a Protestant chaplain. I told him
I would prefer another Catholic chaplain, since half of my personnel
were Catholic. He told me not to worry. He would send me a good
Catholic chaplain as a replacement before we had to leave for
Tinian. I felt like walking on air—not water—after receiving this
good news from the fleet chaplain.

Later, when I returned to see Neil Kingsley to thank him for
his help in the chaplain matter, he told me that a small female
troupe was performing for the USO at Schofield Barracks, an army
installation north of Pearl. One of them was Dorothy Fay Ritter,
Tex Ritter's wife. We went up and enjoyed the show and then went
backstage for a visit with Dorothy Fay and her troupe. We had a
nice reunion and then dinner with Cmdr. Kingsley. Dorothy Fay
told me they were due to go to Kwajalein next with the show and
would report to General Tenney there. I told her to alert me when
she arrived at Kwajalein so we might make plans for her troupe to
entertain my battalion on Bigej Island.

When I reported to DIRPACDOCKS for briefing on our move to
Tinian, I was told of the earlier plan to take the 107th off the ship
at Pearl and substitute a battalion on Red Hill as a replacement.
The captain in charge of the office there wondered how it happened
that we slipped through. They were waiting for us—and we never
showed up. The next thing he knew, we were in Kwajalein, and
it was too late to make the exchange of battalions. I evaded this
inquiry by saying that I just followed orders from my immediate
superior, the C.O. of Acorn 23. My explanation was accepted and
the subject dropped.

I had received a fine briefing at DIPRACDOCKS regarding prep-
arations I should undertake in anticipation of an early departure

to Tinian, and the nature of our mission at our next Island X. I was told that we would be initially quartered in tents with coral floors, since no wood floors would be permitted due to the lumber shortage in the Marianas. On completion of my assignment to Pearl Harbor, I managed a couple of days in Honolulu. I stayed at the Royal Hawaiian Hotel on Waikiki Beach. This fine old hotel [which was 17 years old in 1944] was a navy club and BOQ.[10] It was nice to enjoy these plush surroundings before catching my seaplane back to Ebeye Island. This had been a very successful trip for my battalion.

## Bigej Island

A short while after I returned from Pearl Harbor to the Battalion on Bigej, I had a pleasant surprise. On a rainy, blustery night, a personnel carrier docked at our small pier and deposited a lone passenger and his gear. He was Lt. John Eulberg, a Catholic chaplain, with orders to relieve Fr. Fonash, our present chaplain. He also had a set of orders for Fr. Fonash to return to Pearl Harbor and report to the chief of chaplains, the captain I had contacted earlier. In a few days, Fr. Fonash was detached and caught a flight back to Pearl. I think he was secretly pleased to be free of the 107th— as we were of him. Fr. Eulberg had been with the 13th Seabees, so the chief of chaplains stole him for us. It was a real joy to see how this new chaplain immediately started to get his department in shape. He made it apparent from the beginning that he would be chaplain for the whole battalion. Incidentally, he was a Dominican priest and hailed from Wisconsin.

10. After Pearl Harbor, the Royal Hawaiian was taken over by the navy from 1942 to 1945 and reopened to civilian guests in 1947–20 years after it originally opened. The Moana Hotel next door remained in civilian use, even though the only guests there during the war were military personnel. During the war, most of the military personnel who stayed at the Royal Hawaiian were men from the submarines or "the silent service." Enlisted men stayed for free and officers, such as my grandfather, only had to pay $1.00 a day. My grandfather remembered the view of Diamond Head, with the palm trees on Waikiki, before the postwar tourist redevelopment took place there after statehood in 1959. Stan Cohen, *The Pink Palace: Royal Hawaiian, Waikiki* (Missoula, MT: Pictorial Histories Publishing Company, Inc., 1986, 1999), 52–63.

Early in July 1944, Bob Hope (1903–2003) and a troupe of entertainers [of the USO] came to Kwajalein under the auspices of the army. I was invited along with my officers to attend the show as guests. Since the LCT (landing craft tank) assigned to us was just large enough to transport our officer personnel, with no room for our enlisted people, I declined. I did not feel that it was fair for the officers to go and see Bob Hope while the enlisted personnel stayed on Bigej. So I sent the chaplain and his staff down to Kwajalein to see the show and represent the 107th.

Later in July 1944, I received a message from army headquarters that Dorothy Fay Ritter and her troupe had arrived in Kwajalein to do a show. I had our coxswain drop me off at Ebeye, where Commander Hopf assigned his private speedboat with coxswain to me for the day. I went over to Kwajalein and had a late breakfast with Dorothy and her troupe. Brig. General Tenney (we called him "Straw Hat Tenney," since he always wore a wide brimmed straw hat instead of the regulation army cap) had breakfast with us. Since my battalion had missed the Bob Hope show, I asked permission to have the troupe do a matinee for the 107th on Bigej. The general expressed his regret to have to say no to me, one of his island commanders, but said that two shows in one day would tire the troupe. However, he did consent for me to take them on a speed boat ride up the lagoon for a brief visit to Bigej Island. En route, Dorothy agreed that the troupe could do an impromptu show for us, allowing each girl to dance, sing or recite, according to their individual talents. In this way, they would not do their regular show, which was a comedy play, but would perform for the 107th vaudeville style. Since none of my officers or men were expecting visitors, you can imagine their surprise—and delight— when I stepped ashore from the dock at Bigej followed by five lovely ladies. Despite the fact that none of our personnel had seen a woman since leaving Pearl Harbor, over five months ago, they conducted themselves with remarkable restraint. We gave the girls a tour of the island and permitted them to visit and converse with our personnel. As expected, some found one of the girls from their hometown, so messages were given for the folks back home.

When lunch was served for our female guests, they probably expected to eat at the officers' mess. However, I elected to place them in line as singles with the men in the enlisted mess. This was a popular decision, both for the men and visitors. After lunch, we all went over to our open air theater we had built as a part of the fleet recreation center. Here, the troupe put on a fine show for the 107th. Their individual talents were amazing, and the applause was deafening. After the show and final goodbyes at the dock, I sent the troupe back to Kwajalein in Commander Hopf's speedboat. It had been a gala day—one we would never forget. General Tenney never once mentioned that I had technically violated his orders. Later, this visit was recorded in the 107th logbook under the caption: "Rex Ritter's Critters with Tex Ritter's Gals." This event was the highlight of our stay on the Kwajalein Atoll. I will always be grateful to Dorothy Fay for her contribution to the morale of the 107th Seabees in agreeing to allow her troupe to perform individual acts without any rehearsals.

On August 27, 1944 [two days after the liberation of Paris], I received orders to move the 107th Battalion to Tinian in the Marianas. I had been expecting these orders since my return from Pearl Harbor. We were told the "cube" allowed for our gear on the three LST's (Landing Ship Tanks) being assigned to transport us to Tinian. A portion of our people had been very busy "palletizing" tent materials, which would be set up in Tinian for quarters, messing and administration. The tent gear was packed in 8 × 8 plywood crates. In this way we saved hold spaces on the LST's—and insured having prefab floors for our tent city. In addition to regular 16 × 16 pyramidal tents for quarters, we had other designs for mess halls, offices and even a small chapel. By utilizing this packing technique, we would avoid the coral floors prescribed on Tinian due to the shortage of lumber.

We hurried to complete our mission for the fleet fuel farm and recreation center in order to be ready to load our LST's on arrival at Bigej. The marine contingent under my command on Bigej gave our men intensive military training, especially in rifles and mortars. We fully expected to see some combat on our arrival in Tinian.

On September 1, 1944 [five years to the day after World War II began], we loaded out the three LST's and the 107th said goodbye to Kwajalein Atoll as they sailed out through the South Pass. I placed my exec, Lieutenant McKay in charge, since I had elected to fly to Tinian in order to arrange for speedy debarkation and unloading on arrival at our next Island X. I went by Ebeye Island and said goodbye to all my old friends. Then I went over to Kwajalein to say goodbye to General Tenney and his staff and boarded a DC-3 for Tinian. It had been six months since we arrived at the Kwajalein Atoll, and I found I was proud of the job my battalion had done on this—our first Island X. As I was flying out, it was amazing to reflect on all the jobs we had completed in such a short period of time. I had complete confidence in my battalion's ability to perform in a similar admirable fashion on Tinian.

# Chapter 6

✦
✦
✦
✦
✦

# 1944: The Central Pacific: Tinian

## *Tinian Island*

I arrived in Tinian early in September 1944. Our plane landed on a field at the north end of the island, just across the channel from Saipan. I was met by Lieutenant Pinkerton, who took me to the 92nd Seabee Headquarters, where I would stay awaiting the arrival of the 107th on the three LST's. On September 5, I reported to the CINC of the 6th Naval Brigade, to which we would be attached.

Tinian Island is in the northern part of the Marianas chain, with Guam to the south and Saipan next door to the north. Tinian is a relatively flat plateau compared to the mountainous terrain of Saipan, which lies across a narrow channel. It is six miles long and three miles wide. The terrain was ideal for constructing bomber strips to accommodate the new B-29s [which became operational in June 1944], which were now replacing the B-24's [Liberators], which had made aviation history in the European sector. The climate is similar to Hawaii, and the trade winds keep the weather relatively cool. It rains almost every day. Also, hardly a day passes that we do not have a small earthquake. No one seems to pay any attention to these tremors, as they do no damage. The island abounds with sugar cane fields, which the Japanese had cultivated

with indentured Okinawan labor. There was a large sugar mill in
Tinian Town, which had been devastated by our bombers and fleet
units. Taros, a tuberous root similar to our yams, grow here in
abundance.[1]

Tinian was assigned to the Japanese as a League of Nations
Mandate at the end of World War I [from 1919–1944], with the
condition that no military facilities would be installed. As was
done on all the other Marianas islands, the Japanese immediately
violated this mandate by fortifying the island and constructing the
strips for fighter planes.[2]

Shortly before my arrival, the U.S. Marines had secured the
island[3] by occupying the narrow waist of the island at Tinian Town.
This action cut the Japanese forces in half and broke communications between the groups; however there were still Japanese forces
in the area of our camp site. Prior to the arrival of the 107th from
Kwajalein in the three LST's, I had arranged logistical support
from the 92nd Battalion to expedite unloading and transporting our
personnel and gear to our campsite. As anticipated, my flying out
ahead paid off.

My battalion arrived at Tinian harbor on September 12, 1944.
The initial support I had arranged from the 92nd expedited the
transfer of our men, equipment and supplies to our campsite with
nary a hitch. We set up a temporary office and command post
under a large tarp on a coral strip that had been a Japanese fighter
strip. We set up our perimeter security and proceeded with surveys
to plan the location of our various base facilities. Our palletizing
program back on Bigej Island really paid off. Personnel quarters with
16 × 16 tents, with wood floors from the crates, were set up rapidly.

1. "Building the airfields at Tinian was just about the biggest single job
the Seabees undertook during World War II." Castillo, *The Seabees of World
War II,* 116.

2. In the Washington Naval Treaty of 1922, which limited Japanese naval
tonnage to a lesser amount than that of the U.S. and Britain, the U.S. agreed to
not fortify Guam and the Philippines. Alexander DeConde, *A History of American
Foreign Policy* (New York: Charles Scribner's Sons, 1963), 498–502.

3. During Operation Forager, or the Mariana and Palau Islands campaign,
from June–November 1944. By the Editors of American Heritage, *The American
Heritage Pictorial Atlas of United States History* (New York: The American
Heritage Publishing Co., Inc., 1966), 296–297.

Very few of our men had to sleep in pup tents, even on our first night ashore. This operation simulated the Barnum and Bailey Circus coming to town. Initially, we subsisted on K rations, but switched to C rations in a couple of days. I preferred the K. I did not like the sloppy stews in the C ration kits. Due to our speed in planning and constructing our facilities, we had our tent galley in operation in less than a week. Then we commenced serving hot meals to our personnel. Earlier units on the island marveled at the speed the 107th showed in getting our permanent camp in operation.

Each night after we arrived, our security patrols had to repel Japanese intruders, who were after food, blankets and even our trucks. It was a new experience trying to sleep, not knowing whether some desperate Japanese might slip into your tent and do you in. The sporadic fire of our patrols kept up a staccato throughout most of the earlier nights after our arrival. After a while, you got used to the noise from the firearms and slept through the turmoil. Fortunately, none of our sentries were ever hurt during the exchange of fire, although we felt that some of the Japanese intruders were wounded by the patrols.

Thanks to our planning and speed of camp construction, we were able to beat the deadline set for us by the brigade commander for getting settled and available for work assignments on our mission. Our battalion office was a 16x16 tent in the middle of our camp. I shared this office with my exec. We also set up an attractive tent chapel for Father Eulberg. "Officer's Country" was a row of tents in what had been an Okinawan village. This was the only part of our camp that had shrubs and trees. The rest had been carved out of a sugar cane field. McKay and I shared a tent at the end of the row attached to our tent home. In the evening, Mac and I could sit out on our porch, enjoy the cool breezes, and observe the sex lives of the papaya. You see, one of the trees was male—the other female. The male had the blossoms and the female had the fruit. We even learned to like the aromatic flavor of the papaya for breakfast. We constructed usable roads throughout the camp from a coral quarry nearby. We were one of the few units that had wood floors in our quarters—thanks to our palletizing scheme back in Bigej. My superiors thought we had cheated on the no wood floor policy, but agreed that we had not used any island lumber—which was in short supply.

Our island commander was a brigadier general in the Army Air Force. [Navy] Capt. Paul J. Halloran was the OINC of the 6th Naval Construction Brigade. He was a New Yorker and named the streets from those in Manhattan, such as Broadway, 5th Avenue, Riverside Drive, etc. "Wild Pete," as he was often referred to, could be a bit difficult. His exec. Commander Hartman was a former officer at Port Hueneme and I knew and liked him there. He was a good man to know. He helped me through several tight spots in my relations with the brigade. My immediate superior was Commander Neely, OINC of the 29th Regiment. His exec was Lieut.-Cmdr. Joe Barnwell from South Carolina, so he and I spoke the same language. "Doc" Neely ran a construction company in Philadelphia before the war. He was a fine and gentle person.

There was a small marine anti-aircraft unit near our camp with their tents on the coral Japanese airstrip. This unit was headed by a captain and a sergeant. I furnished them with some scrap lumber—"dunnage"—to floor their tents and invited them to join our mess. Commander Neely came to see me about adopting this marine unit and asked by what authority I had done so. I explained that they would have stolen our food—and even our plywood—if I had not invited them into our facilities. As our guests, they would not want to steal from us. Marines have a reputation of "procuring" anything that is not nailed down. Every marine is his own supply officer. They would also provide us with the additional security from Japanese raids on our camp. "Doc" Neely agreed that I had shown good judgment in taking care of the marines.

The primary purpose of construction battalions on Tinian was to build airstrips (runways) and supporting facilities for bomber groups to send our new B-29 [Superfortress] bombers on raids to Japan and other enemy positions. The largest single jobs were runways—seven in all, 7,000 feet in length—were under construction. There were five separate Seabee battalions on the island by the time we were being given assignments. The runways were the largest single jobs and required the road-building capabilities of several battalions. I tried to avoid being assigned to runway construction, since my people would be fragmented and often under the command of officers and chiefs from other battalions. I figured this could create a morale problem for my men. So, I managed to get assigned to single jobs, such as taxiways and roads that my men could handle alone under the leadership and command of their own officers and petty officers. This was a wise move, since the productivity of our own battalion could be measured. We were also able to maintain our identity by not being merged with the other battalions.

The executive officer of the 29th Regiment, Joe Barnwell, often had the distasteful job of recruiting working parties for unloading ships, cleanup crews and other jobs common to the island. I tried to discourage having to send my people for these extraneous assignments under the leadership of others. Joe and I understood each other, and I knew he had been ordered to find men for these working parties, so I usually lost and had to comply with the order. Then I noted that my exec, Howard McKay from Philadelphia, could avoid these assignments with clever "double talk," so I referred these requests to McKay. We managed to avoid most of them. In the meantime we managed to be assigned to many individual jobs that kept all our personnel very busy meeting the deadlines. We took on base roads, like Riverside Drive, along the western perimeter of the island. This way we avoided having our people fractured into island jobs.

Then we were assigned to a large camp project next door to our base. This involved erection of Quonset huts for housing, messing and administration for a new B-29 bomber group that had just arrived from India [part of the CBI Theater]. Over there they had been flying B-24s over the "Hump" [from India] to China. Their C.O. was Brig. Gen. Roger Ramey (1905–1963). He was originally from Denton, Texas, and had made quite a reputation during his stay in India. His aide, Lt. Col. Jenkins, spent a lot of time in our camp as liaison for General Ramey. In fact, he took many of his meals with us. Our food was better, since we could bring it in by ship, and their liquor was better, since they could fly it in—so I did most of my drinking with them. General Ramey would also have dinner at our officers' mess frequently. He appreciated the job we were doing for his bomber group and did not resent the fact that we were eating better. The reason for this was twofold: First, I had a commissary officer, Lieutenant Heflin, from Houston. He had been a storekeeper on navy carriers before he became an officer. He knew how to get fresh meat and vegetables from navy ships that came into Tinian Harbor. When they came in, he would have a reefer truck on hand to obtain the frozen meat and vegetables. He was uncanny at this procurement. The other factor was the commissary steward, cooks and bakers, whom I had procured before we left the States. Our real prize was "Rene," a French baker we had found in Camp Parks. He made great bread and pastries. We had to "soft pedal" our gourmet fare or would have been deluged with visitors from other units.

Thanks to the foraging abilities of our commissary officer, Lieutenant (j.g.) Heflin, we were able to eat better than our neighbors. We often had fresh meat, while many units, including the bomber group across the road, were still on spam. Once the island commander called me into his office. He had heard that our mess was superior to our neighbors. He said he did not mind—however, we should "soft pedal" this fact, so he would not have to answer complaints from the less fortunate. Lt. Col Jenkins, aide to General Ramey, C.O. of the bomber group, spent many hours with us, particularly at our bar. Somehow, he felt he should repay us by regaling anyone present with "hoary" jokes. Somehow no new jokes got this far in the Pacific. Often he would preface his jokes with: "Don't stop if you have heard this one before—I want to hear it again myself." Which was one of the best lines I had heard lately. Jenkins and his sister ran a Dude Ranch south of Tucson before he went into the Army Air Forces.

There was a period when we were tormented by flies and mosquitos in our camp. The same problem existed in other units on Tinian. The flies came from the sugar cane fields nearby, and the mosquitos from stagnant pools in the vicinity. Captain Halloran sent fly and mosquito traps to all Seabee units on the island. These pests brought on a siege of dengue fever, which incapacitated many of our working personnel. The captain ordered these traps to be put to full use. In the meantime, our senior medical officer found two entomologists in our battalion, who had had experience in fly and mosquito control in the Tennessee Valley Authority (TVA). The entomologists simply went to the breeding grounds and destroyed the large larvae with sprays. In a relatively short period, our camp was completely free of these pests. Later, Captain Halloran made an inspection of our camp and noted that we no longer needed the fly and mosquito traps. For a while, our entomologists were in demand from neighbor units. The captain sent me a letter of congratulation for our contribution to pest control on Tinian.

On November 3, 1944 [five days before FDR was reelected the fourth and last time on November 7], we had our first Japanese air raid. They hit our North Field and damaged a B-24 bomber. No one was injured. On November 7, my first wedding anniversary, the Japanese came again and dropped anti-personnel bombs near our camp. Fortunately, no one was hurt, although it was evening and our battalion theater was packed for a movie. After the raid I would order the movie shut off and the theater evacuated after the first alert. Otherwise, many would have strayed into the theater just to hold their good seats, and be open targets for strings of anti-personnel bombs. On November 27, they came again. Our camp took a little flak, but we had no injuries. When the raids occurred, always at night, it was amusing to me to see my exec leave our tent in a big hurry to his foxhole. One night he jumped into the foxhole that was filled with water from recent rains. Either the Japanese were poor gunners—or we were just lucky, since we never had any injuries and suffered only minor damage to our camp.

Just before Thanksgiving 1944, a new battalion arrived to join our regiment. Their mission was waterfront construction, so they were assigned a marshy area near the waterfront and harbor. This unit was the 45th Seabees under Lt. Cmdr. James Marsh. They had been stationed at Midway for some time and had all the comforts of home. Suddenly they were dumped out here, and no one seemed to pay much attention to their arrival. Here they were literally camping out in the marsh and eating K-rations. I noted their desperate situation while the rest of us were comfortably ensconced. I contacted the skipper of the 92nd Battalion, and each of us agreed to invite half of their battalion for Thanksgiving dinner. Lieutenant-Commander Marsh was eternally grateful and insisted that this was the best Thanksgiving ever. It did not take them long to get settled and start work on the waterfront. We always referred to them as the "Gooney Bird" Battalion, because of the prevalence of gooney birds [albatrosses] on Midway Island. Jim Marsh and I have been good friends ever since. He always reminds me of our thoughtfulness on Thanksgiving Day 1944.[4]

On Christmas Day 1944, we presented a special gift box to each man in our hospital. They were surprised—and delighted. Also,

---

4. This was done as an afterthought on page 69 in the original typed memoirs.

we prepared a special edition of our *107*th *Pipeline*, our battalion newspaper, and distributed it to all hands. This issue had been edited so it could be sent home. This pleased our personnel. On Christmas Day I was told that no Protestant chaplain was available to conduct Christmas service for Protestants in the battalion. Father Eulberg, our Catholic chaplain, came to me and volunteered to conduct Protestant services in a chapel on Christmas Day. I demurred, stating that he might be censured. He answered me with: "Skipper, on this island, I am the bishop—and I make the rules." I attended and heard a very fine Protestant sermon from our Catholic chaplain. He was a great guy! This Christmas did not measure up to the previous one [in 1943] at San Jose with my wife and her folks—however it was a good Christmas under these circumstances.[5]

By the end of December 1944, our B-29 bombers were on a regular schedule to bomb the enemy in their homeland.[6] We called it the "Empire Run." We had now completed three 8500- foot runways for them to take off, with a full bomb load, headed for Japan.[7] It was an unforgettable sight to watch these planes take off at dusk on the "Empire Run." I was always welcomed to join General Ramey in the [control] tower to witness the takeoffs. The planes were so close behind each other that if one had to abort at the last taxiway, the following plane would have to scurry to escape the next plane in line. More than once, I witnessed a crash at the end of the runway, which usually meant that all hands were killed when their plane failed to get airborne. War is a terrible thing when you witness these young men being sacrificed in this manner.

---

5. I have a copy of the *107*th *U.S. Naval Construction Battalion, Merry Christmas, Western Pacific, 25 December 1944*, program.

6. The first B-29 raid from the Marianas took place on November 24, 1944, when 111 B-29s bombed Tokyo. This raid was made into a documentary film called *Target Tokyo* (1945) that was narrated by Lt. Ronald Reagan, USAAF. The 1945 documentary film *The Last Bomb* covers a typical B-29 raid on Japan by mid-1945. In the episode "The Bomb" in *The World at War* series, (1974), Sir Laurence Olivier, who narrated the series, described Tinian as the biggest airbase in the world by 1945.

7. North Field became operational by February 1945.

# Chapter 7

✦
✦
✦
✦
✦

# 1945: The Beginning of the End

Each Seabee battalion on Tinian adopted a particular plane and the crew painted identification on the nose of the B-29. The 107th named their plane "Jackpot." The "Jackpot" made its maiden run over Japan on January 2, 1945. We were pleased to see the results credited to our adopted aircraft after each raid on the Japanese homeland.

It was a sad experience when you lose your first Seabee. You know it is going to happen—but you are never quite ready for it. Early in 1945, Ed Zeph from upstate New York was checking an electric motor which was activating a washing machine for cleaning spare parts for our tractors. A short developed while his hands were in the liquid, and he was knocked out by the shock. We rushed him to the base hospital in our ambulance with a doctor and chaplain along, trying to resuscitate him. We followed a little later, and when I got to the hospital, I was told that Zeph had been moved to another Quonset at the hospital from the emergency room. I walked in, not knowing this Quonset was the morgue, just in time to see the doctors starting to do a post-mortem. This was a sad moment for me, realizing that we had been unable to save him. At the hospital, they gave me his personal effects, including a picture of his wife—a beautiful girl. This was my hardest task to date. This was the first casualty in our battalion in over a year with the 1,080 men and 33 officers. Unfortunately, it would not be our last—but I guess the first one is the hardest to take.

The 107th Battalion had attained a reputation as a unit filled with professional builders. Our completed jobs, for which we received praise, included taxiways, camps, and roads, especially Riverside Drive, around the west side of the island. As an ex-highway engineer, I took pride in the heavy construction work our battalion had accomplished. Now we had a request to build a residence. This house was for one of our favorite people—[USAAF] General Ramey. It was to be built near the army hospital nurses' quarters, north and east of our camp. I elected to do the initial reconnaissance for this job alone. I took a carbine (I had long since given up my .45 automatic for the more dependable carbine) and drove my jeep to the edge of a cane field near the proposed site of the house we were to build. I walked through the cane field toward the site, when suddenly I came upon a hidden area, well camouflaged. I cautiously explored the area and noted items such as army blankets, K-rations, army clothes and an aluminum dish with Japanese instructions on the bottom. Obviously, this was a hideout for Japanese soldiers [who had escaped capture during the Battle of Tinian by hiding]. Suppose they were nearby and would return to their hideout! I sensed the predicament I could be in, so I discontinued my reconnaissance and cautiously made my way back to my jeep. I returned to the camp and made the area I had explored out of bounds, except for personnel assigned to build the house. I also ordered sentries posted in the area while work progressed on General Ramey's house.

A short while later, two young seamen from the 107th decided to explore the area on their day off, although I had made it out of bounds. Two Japanese fired on them. One of our men got away, but the other was hit by one of the shots. The one who escaped reported the incident, and we sent a security patrol to the area. They found Seaman Vaughn Fullwiler's body in the cane field. He was from Roseville, near Sacramento, California.

We lost our second Seabee from Japanese sniper fire in a cane field. We gave Seaman Fullwiler a military funeral and buried him in the military cemetery alongside Ed Zeph, who had died earlier by accidental electrocution. This second death in our battalion seemed so useless—and he died so young. I could not bring myself to punish his companion, despite the fact that he took the young seaman into a forbidden area.

Early in 1945, in addition to the residence we had completed for General Ramey, we tackled three other unusual jobs, as follows:

1.  The Japanese had previously installed a radio tower on one of their fighter strips at the north end of the Island. We volunteered to dismantle this bolted structure and re-erect it on the highest point on the island near the West Field, where there were three B-29 runways. At this point the tower could be used as homing beam for return-ing planes. Incidentally, this type of tower was originally designed by the French.[1] The job was hazardous and took all the rigging skills we could find in our battalion. Lt. (j.g.) "Woody" Eccles, who had his own engineering firm in New Castle, near Pittsburgh, was placed in charge of the opera-tion. On completion we received many plaudits for doing a difficult job. All the top brass on the island joined in the commissioning ceremony.

2.  The 107th had previously erected fuel storage tanks near the harbor of Tinian. Our earlier experiences in building the fuel farm for the navy on Bigej Island on Kwajalein Atoll came in handy. Now we were requested to extend fuel lines out into the bay to connect with buoys where tanker ships tied up. This would permit fuel ships to discharge directly into the storage tanks we had installed earlier. Warrant Officer Carl Gunther from Indianapolis was placed in charge of this project. He devised a plan to fabricate three fuel lines (gasoline, diesel, and aviation fuel) on the shore and then push them out to sea to the buoys by using several D-8 tractors. Empty oil drums were used to float the lines as they were being slowly pushed out into the bay. Everything

---

1.  The Eiffel Tower was used as a radio tower. The old RKO films featured a picture of radio waves coming out of the tower, calling themselves "RKO Radio Pictures." Ironically, the tower "was not to everyone's taste" and "was supposed to be dismantled after 20 years; it survived only because the large radio antenna that was later bolted to it was vital to French radio telegraphy." Brian Moynahan, *The French Century* (Paris: Flammarion, 2007), 35.

went smoothly, and the three lines were safely attached to the tanker buoys. There was quite a celebration when the final connections were made and the fuel started coming ashore from a tanker in the buoy to our storage tanks. This was just one more example of the ingenuity demonstrated by personnel in the 107th.

3.   The old Japanese sugar mill near the main harbor in Tinian was a tangled mess of ruins, due to our shelling and bombing during the assault phase. The steel frames were dangling and presented a hazard to anyone who might venture into the vicinity. The 107th volunteered to demolish the old structure and salvage any usable steel for other projects on the Island. Lt. (j.g.) P.O. Spalding, from Portland, Maine, was placed in charge of this hazardous undertaking. Due to his careful planning and execution by our riggers, the project was completed in record time with only a few minor injuries to our personnel. These three unusual assignments earned the battalion praise and prestige from our superiors—and gave our men a real boost in morale.

Several times during early 1945, I had the pleasure of dining with captains of navy and civilian ships that came in from San Francisco. This was made possible by suggestions from the Port Director in San Francisco, Capt. Will Peterson (he and his family were good friends of my wife, Jeannette). The visiting captains would bring me word first hand from Jeannette, as delivered by Captain Peterson. One dinner aboard a civilian ship I remember vividly. The captain of the ship told me that Captain Peterson had told him that if he did not have me to dinner, he need not come back to San Francisco. He was a jovial host and served a fine dinner with a very professional steward. I was so impressed that I asked if it would be proper for me to tip his steward. He replied that it was all right but that he did not recommend it, saying: "He makes more money than you do." Later I checked the pay scales for civilians in the war zone and found that he did make more money than a lieutenant commander. I had several pleasant dinners, including one with a navy captain on a supply ship who had met my wife in San Francisco. These were pleasant interludes for the skipper of a battalion with many arduous responsibilities.

We were justifiably proud of our chapel in a canvas tent. It was tastefully decorated on the inside—so it was hard to believe you were sitting in a tent. Father Eulberg, our chaplain, and his staff had done an excellent job to make the interior pleasant and attractive. During Catholic services, it was called the "Chapel of St. Anne," and displayed holy paintings, including an excellent one of St. Francis [San Francisco]. Our battalion artist, Michael Lowe, a Jewish lad from New York, did the oil paintings. He had studied art in both France and Italy. He also did many oils depicting the activities of the 107th on Kwajalein and Tinian. Most of his work is permanently recorded in the battalion logbook. My favorite is a painting of the "Prehistoric Monoliths" located near the harbor in Tinian Town. The painting illustrates the size of the monoliths, with sailors standing alongside for comparison. No one knows exactly where these stone columns came from; however, they are not indigenous to the island. You might say that they represent a "junior grade" Stonehenge. Alongside is a stone monument, erected by the Japanese, explaining this marvel. However, no one in our outfit could read Japanese, so I never found out the origin of this prehistoric structure. It seemed a shame to have this talented artist stoop to do sign painting for roads and buildings, but he was a true Seabee and did not seem to mind.[2]

Every Sunday afternoon a "Symphony in Wax" was held in our little chapel. This function was attended by units from all over the island, so it was often hard to find a seat. I rarely missed a session. As skipper, of course, I had a reserved seat. Reed, our musical director, conducted the sessions, including a narration preceding each rendition. He managed to get good classical recordings from many sources. The "Symphony" always opened with "The Swan of Tuonela" by Sibelius. Reed gave me this record when our battalion was deactivated [after VJ Day in October 1945]. All through the war we managed to keep our band and small orchestra intact under Reed's direction and with the

2. The original painting hung for many years in our family home in San Francisco and now hangs in our home in Virginia. I learned recently from an Air Force officer who had been on Tinian within the past few years that the monoliths were actually supporting structures for the homes of local chiefs hundreds of years ago. He showed me photos on his cell phone, and they were the same structures that were shown in the painting.

support from the Headquarters Company Commander, Lt. Bliss Oliver. My attendance to our "Symphony in Wax" did much to improve my limited musical education. This Sunday event was a highlight throughout the island.

On April 12, 1945, our President and Commander-in-Chief [FDR] died in Warm Springs, Georgia. This was a sad day to lose this great leader [FDR died 26 days before VE Day]. We wondered whether Harry S. Truman could rise to the occasion to replace the great FDR. He did! Fortunately, the war in Europe was almost over, so we should be getting help in the Pacific Area from the European sector. Due to the death of our president, we had our first day off from our work assignments. After this event, we were able to give our people one day off each week. Up to now, we had been on a seven-day schedule. Since we were ahead of schedule, we were able to start a recreation program. We had baseball, boxing and tennis. No golf! I threw out the first ball to inaugurate the season for our inter-company games. We also opened a beer garden and allowed our U.S. Marine neighbors to join the club.

Now we were able to have USO shows in our own theater. The outstanding one was headed by the cowboy star, Gene Autry (1907–1998). He had a professional troupe that put on a well-organized show. Later, at our bar, I had a nice personal visit with Gene. He told me about seeing Tex Ritter in San Francisco on their way out to the Pacific. He and another of his performers sat in the front row of the theater where Tex was performing. Tex did not know they were there. They began to turn the pages of a news-paper to distract Tex during his act. Then, he discovered them and ad-libbed from the stage: "I see I have a couple of jackass friends in the front row trying to heckle me." They had a nice visit after the show. Gene told me he had left Republic Studios to head up USO shows. His spot at Republic was sought by many cowboy actors, including Tex. I heard later that Roy Rogers became Gene's replacement. Too, bad, since Republic spent more on Westerns than any other Hollywood Studio. Just another example of my cousin coming in second again.

During the spring of 1945, we had two important visitors in our camp from our bureau. Rear Admiral Combs, Deputy Chief of the Bureau of Yards & Docks, and Rear Admiral Cotter, Director, Pacific BUDOCKS. They paid us a short visit in company with the Brigade

Commander, Peter Halloran. Rear Admiral Combs had commissioned the 107th at Davisville almost two years ago. It was good to see him again. The last time was in Washington, D.C., when I almost lost the battalion due to my rank [of lieutenant-commander instead of full commander]. Rear Admiral Cotter brought me fresh word from my wife received from his wife, Kay, in San Francisco. Both these senior CEC Officers were ecstatic in their praise of our battalion's performance on Tinian. I never once mentioned that I had not been spot promoted to commander, as had been indicated in Washington after I received my permanent rank of lieutenant-commander. Suffice it to say, I never suffered due to the fact that I was the only battalion OINC with lieutenant-commander rank. All the others on the island were commanders.

On Easter Sunday Father Eulberg could not find a Protestant chaplain to conduct services, so he did the job. He preached a fine Protestant sermon. Also, in the evening he conducted a special mass for the Okinawans on the island. Many of us attended this special mass. These people had been virtual slaves of the Japanese before the war in the cane fields and sugar mill. Now they were free and lived in their own area. Father Eulberg was truly a chaplain for all the battalion—so different from his predecessor.

Right after Easter, Dr. Hurlbut, our senior medical officer, came to me and said something must be done about Father Eulberg. He had anemia and just would not slow down. He went all over the island to say Masses, due to the shortage of Catholic chaplains. Dr. Hurlbut had warned Father Eulberg that if he continued at his present pace, he would either land in the base hospital or be sent back to the States. The father had insisted that work just had to be done and he would take his chances. Then Dr. Hurlbut enlisted my help in this matter. I called the chaplain into my office and told him the situation regarding his health. I asked him to curtail his activities to units on the island for one month. He repeated that the work had to do be done, so he must continue his present pace. He mentioned the shortage of Catholic chaplains on the island—and that he was senior and therefore a "Bishop." In that case, I said, "You are not willing to voluntarily curtail your outside activities?" He insisted that he could not. "In that case," I said, "You are confined to quarters for one week." He flushed with anger and said: "Skipper, you can't do that to me." "I am sorry, Father,"

I said "but I just did." "You are dismissed." For one week, his meals were served to him in his quarters, and he did not leave his tent except to go to the "head." Afterwards, he forgave me for confining him and admitted he felt much better with the week off. Officers are confined to quarters rather than the brig. It is interesting that the chaplain was the only officer out of 32 in the 107th that was disciplined. Dr. Hurlbut was grateful for my action, stating that I probably saved Father Eulberg from pernicious anemia.

In the matter of discipline I had few problems as skipper of a battalion. There were very few ways to get into trouble on this little island. Besides, most of the men were from the construction fraternity and had plenty of the same work they had done in civilian life. I did have a few to captain's mast for minor offenses, such as insubordination. They were usually given warnings, which were removed from their jackets after 90 days. We had one playboy from the Chicago area who liked the limelight. One bright morning our chief master-at-arms brought this fellow, Norman Joseph, to mast. The charges were that he had been caught cooking eggs in the officer's mess at midnight. "Why did you do this foolish thing, Norman?" I asked. He replied without batting an eye: "Skipper, I was hungry." I could hardly contain myself, but when I regained my composure, I gave him the usual warning and told him that if I saw him again at mast before 90 days, I would throw the book at him. Later he became one of my most trusted men to carry out special assignments. Like Father Eulberg, he forgave me for the discipline.

As mentioned earlier, I felt that the two most important items in maintaining morale in the war zone are good food and good mail service. We were fortunate that we had recruited good cooks and experienced mailmen back in the States. We always seemed to have better mail service than the other battalions on the island. Our two mailmen really worked at their job—and it paid off. As to food, we had real professionals in our galley. For example, we had recruited a French baker, named Robert Rene, from Camp Parks Station Force. He was a fine bread and pastry chef—and our people really enjoyed the fruits of his labor. One day, a redheaded hospital corpsman persuaded Rene to go with him to the North Field where "Red" assured him they could get a ride in a B-29 plane. I had issued strict orders that none of our people could go on a combat mission. However, they found a B-29 that was going out on a test run after being repaired (combat damage). At the last minute the captain of the plane agreed to take one of them. Red gallantly stepped aside and let Rene take the test flight. The plane took off, had a mechanical failure, and plunged into the channel just short of Saipan. Red felt guilty and did not come forward when word came to us about the tragic accident. Fortunately, there was one survivor, who verified that our man Rene was aboard, and lost with all the others. None of the bodies were recovered. So now we had lost number three. We were unable to give Rene the military funeral we had given the first two, so we settled for a memorial mass in our chapel. It was clearly evident that the wrong man had died. Red was the instigator and should have been aboard the plane instead of Rene. Fulwiller's companion led him to his death from the sniper. One might say that we were lucky to lose only three men in the two-year period since the battalion was formed—but it was sad to lose these young men—and in each case it seemed so useless. We would miss our prized French baker.

One day in late spring 1945, I had a surprise visit from a chief in the 121st Seabees, attached to the 30th Regiment on Tinian. Jeannette had written that her friend, Signe Walker, also a teacher, had a husband, Jimmy Walker (not the former New York Mayor) with the Seabees on Tinian. I had assumed he was an officer, so I got in touch with him and invited him to come over for lunch and a visit. When he arrived I saw that he was a chief petty officer, but rather than send him to the chiefs' mess for lunch, I waited until my officers had finished lunch and then I took him to the officers' mess as my guest. Jimmy was duly impressed and wrote his wife, Signe, in glowing terms of the VIP treatment he received from me.

Later, I had a surprise visitor from Saipan, Lt. Steve Luce with the 101st Seabees. He was a former associate in the Highway Department at Wichita Falls and one of my favorite young engineers. He was a graduate of Texas Tech and had a charming redheaded wife, Lena. In fact, it was Steve's brother Bill who was indirectly responsible for my getting a commission in the Civil Engineering Corps of the Navy. I saw Steve once more when I visited his unit on Saipan. They moved out shortly afterwards with other groups to Okinawa. It was good to see someone from home again.

Speaking of former associates, Lieutenant Commander Cooper was executive officer of the 67th Seabees on the east side of Tinian.

He and Ray Peppin were the first officers I had met when I reported to Camp Allen, Norfolk, Virginia, for my first duty in the spring of 1942—over three years earlier. Cooper was the one who told me that he wanted "to get this damn war over with and get back to his mules." (He had a farm in Mississippi.) Out here he had a wild skipper who made him stand night watches and still expected him to do his executive officer duties during the day. All this was verified to me by Lt. Larry Wise in the unit. I first met Larry in Kodiak, along with Norm Martinsen, on my way back from the Aleutians. One night, the 67th Battalion was changing the guard at an ammunition dump in their area, when all the guards were surprised and killed by roving Japanese renegades. Coop's skipper blamed him for the incident and gave him a severe reprimand. Then he came to me with his problem. He wanted to get out of his unit. He asked me if I could help him. He did not dare try for a transfer through his skipper.

My old friend Lieutenant-Commander Cooper had confidence I could help him get out of his battalion. Anyway, I had my Yeoman Winans prepare a letter, for his signature, requesting a transfer. To my surprise, the request was honored by the Brigade Commander, Commodore Halloran. However, Coop was not sent back to the States, as he had hoped, but to another Seabee unit on Iwo Jima, a real hot spot following the famous marine assault a short while before [during the Battle of Iwo Jima in February–March 1945]. So my friend Cooper, with my help, was able to escape the skipper of the 67th, but was still a long way from his farm in Mississippi.

Later, in the spring of 1945, I made my first trip to Guam. General Ramey flew me down with him and his sergeant in his private plane. It was a two-motored craft which he flew quite smoothly; however, when we landed in Guam, he bounced on the runway a couple of times before coming to a landing. I observed to him that the flight was great but the landing was a little scary. He replied: "Rex, it was a good landing—you walked away from it, didn't you?"

We visited the Army Air Force headquarters [20th Airforce] and there I met the famous General [Curtis E.] Lemay (1906–1990), [called "Ironpants" by some]. Since we had been losing some B-29's to anti-aircraft fire over Japan, he decreed that we fly much lower to get under their radar screen—and thus surprise them. General Ramey tried to dissuade him, but Lemay insisted his plan was safer. Subsequent events proved General Lemay was right, as we lost fewer planes.[3] He surprised both General Ramey and me by telling us that top-secret plans were afoot for a mass invasion of the Japanese mainland—and our units were included in the plan. Later, General Ramey and I commiserated on the fact that our officers and men all felt sure that they would be relieved shortly by units from Europe and would be going home for rest-and-recreation ("R-and-R"). We both had to keep the plan under our hats and not even tell our executive officers—perhaps in the hope that something would happen to change the plan [which turned out to be the atomic bombs].

Shortly after we returned to Tinian, I was called to brigade headquarters and given secret orders. The 107th was due to land at the tip of Kyushu on D-4 [four days after the start of Operation Olympic on November 1, 1945.][4] Naval intelligence inferred that this would be the hot spot at the south end of the Japanese mainland. [By mid-1945, the Japanese were building up their defenses there for *Ketsu-Go*, the battle plan for the final defense of Japan against a U.S. invasion.] The secret that I carried was doubly hard, when McKay, my exec, the chaplain and other battalion officers kept telling me how great it would be to go back to the states for "R-and-R" in the near future. In the meantime, the men

3. The B-29s had begun low level incendiary raids, starting with Tokyo on March 9–10, 1945, in Operation Meetinghouse, which killed 100,000 Japanese. The firebombing raid on Tokyo was the deadliest of the entire air war, comparable to Hamburg, Dresden, and Hiroshima. The largest B-29 raid on Japan was on August 2, 1945—five days before the atomic bombing of Hiroshima. Norman Polmar, *The Enola Gay: The B-29 That Dropped the Atomic Bomb on Hiroshima* (Washington, D.C.: Brassey's Inc., and the Smithsonian National Air and Space Museum, 2004), 11. Between March and July 1945, the B-29 bombing campaign destroyed 60 medium to large Japanese cities that contained munitions factories and military compounds. Don A. Farrell, *Tinian and the Bomb* (Tinian, MP: Micronesian Productions and University of Guam Press, 2018), 245.

4. Operation Olympic would have been larger than the D-Day invasion of Normandy in June 1944. Olympic was designed to lead to Operation Coronet, the invasion of Honshu, in 1946. We now know that Olympic was being reconsidered and might not have gone forward, based on new Allied intelligence about the strong Japanese defenses on Kyushu in early August 1945. See *Victory in the Pacific*, *American Experience*.

were working harder than ever to finish our assignments in order to go home for a visit, as was so freely predicted by the ever present "scuttlebutt" (navy rumors). Their assurances in this regard made me feel more like a criminal, since I was the only person in the battalion that knew we were not going home from Tinian but to Japan [as it appeared in the spring and summer of 1945].

May 8, 1945 was VE Day. The war in Europe was over. There was great rejoicing and high hopes throughout the battalion. More than ever now, they felt that Seabee battalions would be returning home from Europe for R-and-R and then would come over to relieve us—but I knew better.

## Sydney, Australia

Early in July 1945, my next door neighbor, General Ramey, invited me to join a small group of officers and non-coms he was sending on R-and-R to Australia[5] on one of his B-29's. I requested permission from my immediate superior, Cmdr. "Doc" Neely, to accompany the group and for official orders to make the trip. He was reluctant to grant my request due to the precedent this might set for others in his regiment. So I asked Brigadier General Ramey to use his personal influence with Commander Neely on my behalf. He acceded to the general's request for me to make the trip, but he gave me the strangest orders I have ever received. The orders told me to report in person to General Ramey for such duty as he might assign. With this dubious set of orders, I boarded the B-29 with the others going on to Australia. The first night we flew high over New Guinea, which was still under Japanese control [the part of the island that Douglas MacArthur had bypassed during his campaign on his way to the Philippines in 1943–1944]. Early next morning we landed at Cairns on the northwest corner of Australia. We had breakfast at the airport. The waitress asked me: "Have you had your 'staik' and 'ayegs' yet?" with her typical Aussie accent. The breakfast was great, as was the large glass of whole fresh milk— which I had not had lately. Later we took off and flew to Brisbane,

5. There were about 150,000 Americans based in Australia in 1942–1943, before their rapid reduction in force in 1944 during the Japanese retreat across the Pacific. David Reynolds, *Rich Relations: The American Occupation of Britain 1942–1945* (New York: HarperCollins and Phoenix Press, 1995), 432.

where we spent the night in a hotel. Man—this was really living again! Next morning we took off for Sydney. I would have liked to have stayed longer in Brisbane. It is a charming city.

It was a short flight in our B-29 from Brisbane to Sydney. We arrived in Sydney around the middle of July 1945. When we landed at the airport we drew special attention from onlookers. Apparently, few B-29's had been here before. A couple of naval officers came to the plane to greet me—another naval officer. They proposed to take me in tow and put me up in navy quarters. Considering the dubious set of orders under which I made this trip and General MacArthur's dislike for naval officers invading his private domain, I thought it best not to go with these naval officers. I told them I was under special orders from Brigadier General Ramey, an Army Air Force officer (which was technically true!), and I would have to stay with the other air force officers at the Hotel Australia. I preferred not to expose the set of orders I was carrying and besides, I felt more comfortable with the people I had flown down with. Later, I was happy with this decision.

First, we "logged in" at the air force headquarters. The commanding officer here assigned one of his Aussie secretaries to each of us to act as a guide during our stay in Sydney. The plan was to pick the secretaries up at the office after work, and they would act as our guides around the city and accompany each of us to dinner. Next, we were quartered in separate rooms at the old Hotel Australia, in the heart of Sydney. It was nice to have a comfortable hotel room, all to myself, after camp life in Tinian for many months.

One of the air force officers who came down with us was a full colonel. He was our senior officer; however, we did not have to worry about him. He was quickly adopted by a rich widow and her daughter, who had a suite in the hotel. He moved in with them, drank their booze, and ate most of his meals in their suite. He was a very interesting fellow. He was one of the last of the old cavalry officers in the army and had transferred over to the Army Air Force during the war. He was a typical old-line career officer. I had the pleasure of sharing free drinks at several cocktail parties in the suite during the week we were in Sydney.

The secretary assigned to me as a guide was an intelligent and attractive young woman named Heather Jamieson. Under her guidance I was able to see the sights of Sydney, including the beautiful harbor (more attractive than ours in San Francisco), the famous steel cantilever arch bridge across the channel [opened in 1932], the race track (they practically close down the city on Sundays to attend the races), the Zoo [one of the world's finest with animals in native style habitats, which was ahead of its time in the 1940s], and several fine restaurants for dinners [near the site of the Sydney Opera House, which was built by the harbor in the 1970s]. She also took me across the famous bridge to her parents' home. She lived at home with her mother and father.

My visit to the home of Heather Jamieson's parents was the highlight of my stay in Sydney. Her father and I hit it off from the start. He was a retired builder (retired prematurely because of the current building material shortage due to the war). He planned to resume his contracting business when the war was over. He was of Scottish descent, although a native-born Australian. He hated the British and said the country needed engineers, like me, to come help break the "stranglehold" the "Limeys" [British] held on them. He encouraged me to come there after the war and join him in the construction business [which never happened since my grandfather returned to San Francisco after the war]. He was a very interesting and intelligent fellow.

In addition to his daughter, he had a son who was a major in the Australian Army fighting the Japanese in New Guinea [under MacArthur's command]. He had a second son who was a lance corporal in the army. He was home on sick leave, so I got to meet him. He was a very personable young man. Heather told me her younger brother had leukemia, and the army had sent him home to die. I felt sad about his terminal condition; however, the family seemed reconciled to the fact he would not recover and were happy to have him home for his last days. This was the one unpleasant note during my stay in Sydney. After the visit to her parents' home, Heather drove me back to the Hotel Australia over the beautiful Arch Bridge.

The week in Sydney passed all too quickly for us on this delightful R-and-R. Now we had to board our B-29 for the long, difficult flight back to Tinian. We practically had to drag our colonel out of the widow's suite in the hotel. He had found a home there and would have preferred to retire from the Army Air Force and stay in Sydney. We loaded our plane with fuel and made the flight back to Tinian, over New Guinea, with a fuel stop in Guam. This had been a pleasant respite from my responsibilities in Tinian. I only hope that someday I might be able to return to the beautiful city of Sydney, Australia [My grandfather never did].

## *Tinian and the End of the War*

When I returned from Sydney I found that my battalion had celebrated the second anniversary of our commissioning back in Davisville, RI. They enlisted the help of Commander Neely, my immediate superior, to preside over this event in my absence. He also presented a Presidential Unit Citation to one of our petty officers, who had recently joined the 107th. The citation was for a unit he had previously served with during the Normandy landings [D-Day]. Commander Neely also praised the 107th Battalion for the magnificent contribution we had made during our stay in Tinian. The officers and men were still glowing over the celebration of our second anniversary as a battalion.

I found it difficult to get back into the swing of things after my delightful R-and-R in Sydney. However, while I was away, a tin containing a gourmet cheese came by delayed mail from Jeannette. When I opened the tin, the stench was overpowering. I told McKay I thought the cheese had spoiled due to the delay in transit from San Francisco and we would have to dispose of it. He suggested that we call in Warrant Officer Fred Becker from Wisconsin for an expert opinion. Fred gave the cheese a thorough examination, and finally, with great reluctance, he tearfully said "Skipper, I think we will have to give this cheese a military funeral." He said it was a fine cheese, but just did not make the crossing of the Pacific.

Near the end of July 1945, an incident happened at our North Field which caused great excitement—and started feverish "scuttlebutt." A B-24 plane crashed on the runway, turned over and caught fire. After the fire was extinguished, a lone person was found in the plane. Since the body was badly burned, it was difficult to identify the nationality of the person. An early theory was advanced that the Japanese had sent one of our captured B-24's with a Kamikaze pilot to crash land on this air strip on Tinian, explode the bomb aboard, and wreak severe damage to our facility. No bombs exploded and there was only minimal damage to our North Field. However, great speculation persisted that the Japanese could fly in one of our old planes.

A few days after the B-24 crashed landed on our North Field, causing much speculation regarding possible enemy involvement, our intelligence came up with the true story. This B-24 was one our planes flying out on a reconnaissance flight north of Tinian. When the plane developed engine trouble, the captain ordered all hands to abandon the plane and hit the parachutes before an almost certain crash into the Pacific off Iwo Jima. Apparently, a gunnery sergeant hid out in the tail section instead of jumping with the rest of the crew. Although he had no training in flying the plane, he evidently managed to keep it aloft and tried to land on our North Field. He almost made it! None of the personnel who bailed out were ever rescued—they obviously perished at sea. The captain of the B-24 made a serious mistake in judgment.

Just after the above-mentioned bizarre incident took place, the USS *Indianapolis*, one of our cruisers, quietly sailed [from San Francisco] into the harbor at Tinian [on July 26, 1945]. She quickly discharged some secret cargo [the atomic bomb] and sailed for Guam.[6] Shortly after leaving Guam on her way to Okinawa, the *Indianapolis* was torpedoed [on July 30] by a Japanese sub [*I-58*], with the loss of the ship and most of her crew.[7] Since there had been no evidence of enemy subs in that area for many months, speculation arose with us on Tinian as to what this ship was delivering to our island that was important enough for the Japanese to think the ship still had important cargo aboard—and make them desperate enough to destroy it.

It did not take long for us to piece this puzzle together. [Actually, the Japanese knew nothing about it.] One of our neighbor Seabee battalions drew an assignment to open up a cave near the beach in an isolated area. Then they transported some highly secret gear into

6. The Seabees of the Sixth Naval Construction Brigade helped with the unloading of the atomic bomb components after the *Indianapolis* arrived in Tinian. (https://www.history.navy.mil/research/library/online-reading-room/title-list-alphabetically/s/seabee-history0/world-war-ii.html)

7. Of the 1,195 crewman who were aboard the *Indianapolis*, approximately 900 who survived the sinking died from thirst and shark attacks. In all 879 of the ship's crew died during and after the sinking. Only 316 survivors were left when they were rescued on August 2. The *Indianapolis* was discovered in 2017. Robert D. Ballard, *Graveyards of the Pacific: From Pearl Harbor to Bikini Atoll* (Washington, D.C: National Geographic, Odyssey Enterprises, 2001), 229–232.

the cave, where a special team that came in on the *Indianapolis* proceeded to assemble this gear. Right away, we all knew that this was a very special device and not just a conventional bomb that the *Indianapolis* had delivered. No one in authority was speculating; however, General Ramey, my friend across the road from us, told me that he thought the Japanese were in for a real surprise.[8]

8. On July 25, 1945, during the Potsdam Conference, President Truman had authorized the air force to proceed with the plan to use the atomic bomb on Japan. On July 31 Truman gave the final go ahead with the condition that the bomb should be released "when ready but no sooner than August 2." David McCullough, *Truman* (New York: Simon & Schuster, 1992), 448.

# Chapter 8

✦

✦

✦

✦

✦

# The End of the Pacific War

O n the morning of August 6, 1945, everything seemed
normal on the island of Tinian. The usual squadron of
B-29's had taken off the night before on their routine
Empire Run. However, later in the morning, General Ramey
contacted us with the word that some interesting news was
beginning to come into his headquarters. He asked me to quietly
come over and join him in the radio room. I was sitting there
alone with the general when the initial report came from the
*Enola Gay*, one of our B-29 bombers.[1] This plane had carried a
special bomb and had just dropped it on Hiroshima. Their report
indicated that the devastation was awesome and unbelievable.
After a quick look at the effects of the bomb they had dropped,
they headed back to Tinian.[2]

Now I know what the *Indianapolis* had dropped off earlier
at Tinian, and also why she had been tailed by a Japanese sub
in the normally peaceful waters off Guam [because it was a U.S.

1. The 509th had arrived on Tinian in May 1945 and the *Enola Gay* in early
July. Norman Polmar, *The Enola Gay*, 20, 65.

2. Truman announced the news of the atomic bombing of Hiroshima in a
broadcast from the USS *Augusta. Truman*, 455.

warship—we now know that the Japanese did not know it was carrying the atomic bomb]. We also knew what the team of experts were putting together in the cave that had been opened up by one of the Seabee units. As the work leaked out regarding the secret weapon that had been used at Hiroshima, there was instant speculation that our possession of such a destructive weapon might just bring Japan to her knees.

A couple of nights later, two young officers [of the 509th Composite Group] from the *Enola Gay* came to our officers' mess for dinner. They related the events of their recent mission to Hiroshima. First, they knew they were carrying a special bomb [nicknamed "Little Boy," a uranium bomb], with a special team aboard to direct the dropping. They did not know just what it was. Even the target was not known by the crew—only the pilot [Col. Paul Tibbets (1915–2007)] and the others in the forward cabin knew that. They flew over Hiroshima at a higher level than usual bomb drops— and then dropped this special bomb on orders from the special team. They were told to drop the bomb while approaching Hiroshima and then climb as fast as the plane could manage directly after the release. This was an unusual sequence for this crew that had been on many bombing missions over Japanese cities.

The two officers from the *Enola Gay* told us a scary story about what had happened a few seconds after the bomb was dropped. They said that they had flown in several typhoons on previous B-29 raids, but the updraft from the exploded bomb was the worst storm they had yet encountered. For a while, no one thought the plane could escape from the terrific storm they had caused. Finally the pilot got the plane back to normal, and they flew high over Hiroshima as the smoke cleared. To them, the destruction that the bomb had brought was unbelievable. Then the *Enola Gay* returned to its base on Tinian.[3]

---

3. The *Enola Gay* has been restored to its 1945 appearance and is now on display at the Smithsonian's National Air and Space Museum extension at the Steven F. Udvar-Hazy Center, near Dulles International Airport in Northern Virginia, 28 miles from Washington, D.C., which opened in 2003. During the plane's restoration after the 1980s, it became embroiled in the planned controversial exhibit at the Smithsonian in 1994–1995 for the 50th anniversary of the atomic bombings. The exhibit was cancelled and replaced by a non-political exhibit running from 1995 to 1998, which became one of the most popular exhibits at

Later the special team confirmed that this special bomb had been assembled in the cave in Tinian from parts brought in by the *Indianapolis.* The bomb had been developed under the auspices of the Manhattan Project [one of most the secret projects, next to the Ultra intelligence, in World War II]. The bomb had been tested in the White Sands area of New Mexico [on July 16, 1945]. It was identified as an atomic bomb. The principles leading to its creation had been discovered by Albert Einstein, the great German physicist, who had to leave Germany under pressure from Hitler.[4] If Hitler had only known what Einstein could come up with [and hadn't been anti-Semitic], he would never have let him leave Germany—and the war in Europe—now over—might have gone differently. Hitler might not have died [of suicide] in that bunker in Berlin. Anyway, we got the bomb instead of Germany.

Einstein's famous formula concerned splitting the atom with the creation of unbelievable force. The formula $E = MC^2$ where E is energy, M is Mass and C, the constant, is the speed of light (186,000 miles per second). Note that C is squared, which produces the tremendous energy released in splitting the atom, with the subsequent chain reaction. This is why this device could destroy a whole city, such as Hiroshima. It was later explained that Hiroshima was selected since many troops were usually quartered there and many small munitions were produced in practically every home in the city [a kind of feeder system]. How our intelligence arrived at this conclusion is still a mystery to me.

On August 9, 1945, a second atomic bomb [nicknamed "Fat Man," a plutonium bomb] was flown from Tinian and dropped on Nagasaki, where munitions operations were underway. Nagasaki is hemmed in by mountains, and this bomb was not as devastating as the first—however, evidently the results of these two bombs should cause the Japanese government to know that they were dealing with something they would be unable to cope with.[5]

---

the Air and Space Museum in Washington. John T. Correll, "The Smithsonian and the *Enola Gay*," http://www.airforcemag.com, accessed April 2004.

4. Niels Bohr was the other great nuclear physicist who worked on the Manhattan Project.

5. The atomic bombs demolished the *Ketsu-go* strategy—Japan's final battle plan for the Home Islands—along with the Soviet invasion of Manchuria on August 8.

On August 14, 1945 [VJ Day], the Emperor of Japan [Hirohito (1901–1989)] announced the unconditional surrender and sued for peace [August 15 in Japan].[6] To all intents and purposes, this act should end the war—however our earlier experiences with the traitorous acts of the Japanese military command, commencing with the surprise attack on Pearl Harbor and the recent sinking of the *Indianapolis*, led us to wonder whether the Emperor could be trusted to back up his surrender. On Tinian we all hoped for the best, since it was common knowledge that there were only half enough parts left on Tinian to assemble a third bomb. A delay could be expected to obtain delivery of extra parts for another bomb back in the states.

Late in August 1945, General Ramey informed me that there was a mission planned for a large bomber group to circle Tokyo Bay on September 2, 1945, ostensibly to support the planned signing of the [official] surrender.[7] He asked me if I would like to make the trip. I accepted with alacrity, but then asked how he could send me in a combat plane. He said he would sign me on as an assistant gunnery officer.

On September 1, 1945 [six years to the day after Hitler's invasion of Poland had started World War II and one year after my grandfather had left Kwajalein for Tinian], about dusk, I boarded a B-29 as assistant gunnery officer to a 1st lieutenant from Crystal Springs, Texas (near San Antonio—and called the "spinach capital of the world"). This was a regular combat plane with a full load of conventional bombs. You see, our command was not sure that this might not be another Japanese trick, and they might lure us into an attack. Our information indicated that our battleship *Missouri*

6. Truman announced Japan's surrender at 7:00 p.m. Eastern Time on August 14. Hirohito's surrender broadcast was the first time that the Japanese people had heard their emperor's voice. Since 2010, the second Sunday in August has been commemorated as "Spirit of '45 Day" to remember both VJ Day and the Greatest Generation in World War II, which is similar to Pearl Harbor Remembrance Day. On VJ Day, my grandfather remembered how the men in the battalion thought they could go home right away and that he had to remind them they had signed up for the duration, plus six months.

7. The occupation of Japan began on August 28, 1945. General MacArthur arrived on August 30. Keith Wheeler and the Editors of Time-Life Books, *The Fall of Japan* (Alexandria, VA: Time-Life Books, World War II series, 1983), 190.

would be in Tokyo Bay, accompanied by other combat ships, as they would witness the signing.

The B-29, with me aboard as assistant gunnery officer, took off from West Field in Tinian just after dark on September 1. With our heavy load we used every foot of the runway to lift off. Our plane barely cleared the trees on the hillside at the end of the runway. I breathed a sigh of relief as we soared low over the Pacific. The flight was long and a bit dreary. There was no place to stretch out on this combat plane, so I sat up in my chair all night. Our rendezvous point to join the other planes in our bomber group was 100 miles north of Tokyo. Early in the morning of September 2, I sighted the green shoreline of the Japanese coast.

## Tokyo Bay

On September 2, 1945, later to be called VJ Day,[8] we joined the other B-29's in our bomber group, which were already at the rendezvous point and circling. Shortly after that we reached our place in the formation and headed south for Tokyo Bay. We flew overland and the vistas, mountains and forests were magnificent along the Japanese coastline. We saw none of the ravages of war en route. I noted green fields and vineyards—a tribute to the Japanese peasants.

We approached Tokyo Bay from the north and noted the American fleet in full force below. It was easy to spot the [USS] *Missouri*, surrounded by our other combat ships, flying Old Glory. We flew at 4500 feet, and I had a ringside seat overlooking Tokyo Bay. What a thrilling sight this was for me! By now we were convinced that the Japanese really meant to go through with the signing of the truce (official surrender), but we were still alert in the bomber group—just in case of some last minute treachery [the B-29's bomb-bay doors were opened even though there were no bombs loaded in them]. While circling the bay around the *Missouri*, I had a magnificent view of the city of Tokyo and the surrounding area. Mount Fuji, covered with snow, is quite a landmark. It is still an active volcano. I was appalled to see the destruction our raids had

8. Although the first VJ Day was celebrated across the U.S. on August 14–15, Truman had announced that the official VJ Day (September 2) would be proclaimed when Japan formally surrendered to the Allied Powers. (https://www. trumanlibrary.org/publicpapers/index.php?pid=107)

made on the city. Block after block were complete ruins. Nothing was left except for a few tall buildings. Our firebombs had wreaked havoc on a helpless population. There was so little left standing. I noted very little debris—a tribute to the industry of the [Japanese] people. There was one green spot in the heart of Tokyo that stood out like an oasis in a desert. This was the Imperial Palace [or what was left of it], surrounded by a lake.[9]

As the signing time on the *Missouri* drew near, I kept my eyes glued to the deck of this old battlewagon. With my field glasses I could clearly recognize Admiral Nimitz, General MacArthur and the Japanese admiral, who was signing the official surrender [the B-29's and other military planes flying over Tokyo Bay were all part of MacArthur's theatrical ceremony]. It was a great experience for me to witness, first hand, this historic event, even from 4500 feet above [there is a photograph taken on the *Missouri* that shows the B-29s flying over.][10] After the signing, we had hoped to be able to land and look around—but no way. We just began to climb to our cruising altitude, and head home for Tinian. This was as close as I ever got to Tokyo and Japan, but I shall never forget this memorable experience and thank my friend Roger Ramey for this opportunity.[11]

## En route to Tinian

The trip back to Tinian was uneventful initially. We passed low over Iwo Jima and had a good view of the site where the marines raised

9. Although my grandfather implied that the Imperial Palace hadn't been hit, the main palace had been destroyed in a firebombing raid in May 1945 and wasn't rebuilt until 1968. By 1945 Hirohito and the imperial family were living in a bunker on the palace grounds. Wheeler, *The Fall of Japan*, 153; Robert M. Poole, "Japan's Imperial Palace: Beyond the Moat," *National Geographic*, January 2001, 98.

10. The official Japanese surrender on the *Missouri* was recreated on the battleship in 1977 for the movie *MacArthur*, with Gregory Peck in the title role. In October 1945 the *Missouri* took part in the largest Navy Day celebration in the country's history for the returning American fleet in New York City, which was reviewed by President Truman. Since 1999, the *Missouri* has been berthed at Ford Island in Pearl Harbor, a few yards from the USS *Arizona* Memorial, which symbolizes the beginning and the end of the Pacific War. It is now a floating museum and is part of the Pearl Harbor tour. Our family visited the *Missouri* in 2001.

11. My grandfather thought so highly of General Ramey that he named my father after him.

the flag on the hilltop (Mt. Suribachi)—made famous in the photo *Raising the Flag on Iwo Jima* by a San Francisco photographer [Joe Rosenthal (1911–2006), who photographed the raising of the second flag]. I noted the airstrip our crippled B-29's would use on the way back from the Empire Run. After leaving Iwo Jima, I was lying on the deck of the plane in the rear section. Suddenly, I noticed a small fire beneath me. One of the crew put it out with a fire extinguisher. It was just a small electrical fire. Then, I crawled through the "tunnel" to the forward section. I explained to the captain that I came up since they were trying to burn the after part of the plane. He thought this was funny—and invited me to stay with him for the rest of our flight. I had a good view of Saipan and our North Field, before landing at the West Field. This had been a wonderful trip—one I would have hated to miss, but now I was one "tired turkey" after 18 hours aloft with no real place to rest. I thanked the plane captain for a great flight, debarked from the plane and returned to 107th Headquarters, where I went to bed for a long sleep.

### Tinian after the War

After my return from Tokyo Bay to witness the signing of the truce from aloft in a B-29 in September 1945, the 107th worked furiously to complete work already started, primarily on roads, hospitals and the prisoner-of-war (POW) camp in the north end of the island. My people were anxious to complete assignments so, hopefully, they could go home, now that the Japanese had agreed to a truce and the war was over. Now I could tell my exec and the officers in the battalion the secret that I had borne alone. We would not be going to Japan on Operation Olympic, as stated in my secret orders, but would be going home instead. This was a great relief to me to reveal the plan for the invasion of Japan that could now be canceled.

By the end of September 1945, I was allowed to send a few officers and men home on emergency conditions. One of the first was Lieutenant McGill, Commander of Co. D. His wife was quite ill in New Jersey. He was in a bad way and needed to get away from Tinian. Ironically, his wife recovered, but Mac died soon after he returned to his home. I set up "request masts" to hear the pleas of men who thought their case was an "emergency." I was deluged by requests from personnel wanting to be sent home. They concocted every conceivable emergency to justify being sent home. It was my unenviable job to sift the real from the fictitious. One of the men who came to my "request mast" was one of our very capable chief petty officers—Joe Sullivan from San Francisco. He told me there was no one sick at home and no real emergency, except he needed to get back home in time to run for Business Agent of Carpenter's Local #22. If he didn't, someone else would be elected and he would be out in the cold when he returned to San Francisco. I told Joe that I appreciated his honesty, but up to now only emergency cases could be considered. I told him that I had information, if I could trust him to keep it quiet, that in a couple of weeks I would be able to honor his request to be sent home. Later I called him in, with several others, and gave him orders to return to San Francisco. He got back in time to run for and win the office of business agent with his union. After retiring to San Francisco I had the pleasure of seeing Joe many times and noted he became a prominent labor leader until he retired.

The last part of September and early October [1945] were hectic times for our battalion. The men knew the war was over and could not understand why they were not permitted to go home. [As stated earlier, they had signed up for the duration of the war plus six months.] On the other hand, the brigade commander, a career naval officer, was pushing us to complete the work we had started. He was a commodore now and did not mind throwing his rank around, particularly to a lowly lieutenant-commander, like myself. The morale of our men was at its lowest ebb and it took a lot of patience on my part and that of my senior officers to keep things on an even keel.

To add to my problems, I received evidence that our chief corpsman was selling grain alcohol to marines at the POW camp. He had forged Dr. Hurlbut's signature on requisitions to the naval hospital for the alcohol. My legal officer, Lieutenant Welch (Co. B Commander) produced conclusive evidence of the guilt of this chief. I considered this an unforgivable violation of trust by a responsible chief petty officer—an act that endangered everyone's safety by selling the stuff, illegally secured, to marines who were assigned to guard prisoners of war. I requested that he be given a general court martial. My request that the chief be tried by a general court resulted in his being transferred out of the 107th to the naval hospital on the island. Ostensibly, he was assigned there awaiting his trial. To my utter dismay, I found out later that the captain at the hospital just let the matter die. The chief did not deserve to go scot free, even though the war was over. Medical officers in command are unpredictable. Earlier, on Bigej Island, I had given a sailor a bad conduct discharge for stealing. Now this was only the second serious offense I had to deal with in over two years with this battalion of 33 officers and 1,081 men. I consider this a pretty good record for the 107th Battalion.

As the 107th completed each work assignment, I was allowed to give more of our personnel orders to return home—some by air, others by ship—whatever was available. There was never enough available transportation to take care of those who wished to and deserved to go home. Also, I had to detain quite a few men to take care of packing and shipping battalion gear and equipment. Most of our material went by ship to Guam. We were now really in the process of deactivating our battalion that we had commissioned over two years earlier. Final deactivation involves a lot of details—like breaking up housekeeping. Our job was made easier since Lt. Cmdr. Joe Barnwell, executive officer of our 29th Regiment, was staying in the service and would be going to Guam to take over the 103rd Seabees there. We were able to turn over most of the rest of our gear to him for the 103rd on Guam. He was of great assistance in our final deactivation. We shipped several items of interest, such as our oil paintings done by our battalion artist, to Port Hueneme to be placed in the Seabee Museum being established there. [There is a new museum there now.] I kept the painting of the "Prehistoric Monoliths" in Tinian Town. This painting occupies a place of prominence in my den. Joe Barnwell called me one day to advise me that he would take over items such as our battalion library, drafting paraphernalia and several other miscellaneous items. This completed the final disposal of everything associated with the 107th Battalion.

Near the middle of October 1945, Lieutenant Commander Barnwell called to tell me that he had cleared everything with the brigade and that the 107th Battalion was officially deactivated. I had a feeling of sadness to know that the 107th had ceased to exist. My battalion had been formed at Camp Peary, Virginia, on July 13, 1943, and commissioned at Davisville,

Rhode Island, on July 31, 1943. Now I had lost "my baby" after two years and three months association. It would be good to go home and rejoin my wife, but the final loss of the 107th Seabees left a void. It had been a good battalion, and I was proud to have been the skipper.

After receiving official word of our deactivation, I had another call from my friend Joe Barnwell. He asked me to come over to his office and brief him on how to run a battalion. He faced this task in Guam where he would be OINC of the 103rd. I told Joe that I appreciated the compliment, but I remembered he had been running my battalion by telephone for some time—and should know all the answers. However, I admitted I was just being facetious. I went over and sat with Joe and answered his questions relative to the problems he would face as skipper of a battalion. He was deeply appreciative of this gesture on my part.

Earlier, our men in the *Pipeline* office, our battalion newspaper, and those in the chaplain's office, with the help of two photographers, had put together material for a battalion log book. Unfortunately, we did not have enough funds in our welfare fund to finance the publishing of the log of the 107th Seabees [*The Log of the 107th Seabees, 1943–1945: A Story of a Seabee Battalion conceived in war ... Dedicated to peace.*] so we had to charge $10 a copy for the book. Most of our personnel subscribed. Also, the war ended before we were able to get the book published and delivered. Proofs were in the hands of the Army-Navy Publishing Co.—a private firm—in Baton Rouge, LA. Hopefully, delivery of the book to subscribers would come to their homes in the near future. Sometime before, the staff had asked me to write a prologue for the log book. Although I inscribed something hurriedly, as I was quite busy at the time, it is something that I still cherish.

Here is a verbatim quote of the prologue I submitted:

"This is your Log—the record of your Battalion and your activities. Over two years ago, you began to lay the ground work for the team that never quit until the job was done and made every deadline imposed by military necessity.

Now that the job is done, I salute you individually, and express the hope that this volume may serve to remind you of the thrill of accomplishment and the joy of pleasant associations, long after the hardships, frustrations, nostalgia and loneliness have been forgotten.

I shall always be grateful for the privilege of serving as your Skipper and for the rich experiences we have shared in this interlude of our lives."

J.R. Ritter"

After final deactivation of the 107th Construction Battalion, I reported directly to the Commander, 6th Naval Brigade. On October 13, 1945, I received orders from Commander, Marianas (Guam) to be detached from duty with the 6th Naval Construction Brigade and report to a staging center for transportation back to the States. These orders also provided for travel to Camp Wallace (near Galveston, Texas) for release from active duty. This was the nearest separation center to my home of record—Rosenberg, Texas. These orders should work to my personal advantage. Normally, I would expect to land in San Francisco, either by air or sea. Then, Jeannette and I could drive in her car to [my parents'] home in Rosenberg, and then to Camp Wallace for separation—all the while still on active duty. Then I would be entitled to 90 days terminal leave—with pay, which could get me back into [postwar] civilian life—and a job.

Just after receiving my detachment orders to return to the States, I suddenly came down with a bad case of the flu. I had never been a patient in a naval hospital—and I did not want to start now. Naval hospitals receive funds based on "patient days." So I was afraid that my orders might be modified, canceled or delayed. I had a good doctor friend at the naval hospital who came to my rescue. He logged me in and out each day without an official admittance. This way, I was not really a patient there, but I received treatment for my illness, without getting involved. Fortunately, I recovered quickly, and I was able to follow my basic orders. After escaping the "clutches" of the naval hospital in Tinian, I completed my recovery in my quarters. Then I packed my gear (I had shipped my foot locker earlier to San Francisco), and I took a small boat across the channel to Saipan.[12]

---

12. The last USAAF unit on Tinian, the 505th Bombardment Group, left North Field in June 1946, which ended its use as an operational airfield. North Field closed in March 1947. (http://www.members.tripod.com/airfields_freeman/HI/Airfields_W_Pacific.htm#northfield)

## *Saipan*

On October 18, 1945, I reported to the Commander, Naval Base, Saipan, to await available government transportation back to the States. I was sent to a receiving station in a dismal part of the island, far removed from the navy base. After one night in this "concentration camp" with the others awaiting a ride home, I knew this was not the place for me. I contacted my old friend Lt. Cmdr. Steve Gulledge, OINC of the Seabee Maintenance Unit that took care of the navy base. I told Steve to "get me out of here before I go 'stir crazy.'" He immediately sent a jeep to pick up me and my gear and take me to his camp. Incidentally, I had known Steve since Texas Highway days, when he was Resident Engineer at Seguin (near San Antonio). Steve was serving Capt. Jimmie Ware, Commander, Naval Base, Saipan. I had known Captain Ware both at Camp Allen and Camp Peary—so I felt right at home.

Waiting for the so called "Magic Carpet" that would take me back to San Francisco and my waiting wife was made more tolerable here in quarters with Steve. Each morning I would go with him to Captain Ware's office to check on his assignments for the day, and then accompany him to the various jobs his men were doing in the maintenance area for the navy base. This gave me something interesting to do to pass the long days of waiting for transportation back to the states. Also, I could learn more about maintenance engineering, which might come in handy later in my professional career.[13]

In the evenings we would often play poker in Steve's quarters, until one evening I lost $50 in less than an hour. I should have remembered not to play poker with Steve. When he was a Resident Engineer back in Texas, he used to go down to Austin when one of his highway jobs was up for bids. He would usually play poker with contractors at the Stephen F. Austin Hotel and usually take their money, until the State Highway Engineer forbade him to come to "lettings." He felt it did not help the image of the department for one of his engineers to take money from a contractor who might bid in one of Steve's highway jobs.

---

13. It did. In the 1950s my grandfather became the Director of Maintenance for the 12th Naval District in San Bruno, California, just south of San Francisco, a federal civilian position he held until he retired in 1965.

Rather than indulge in any more poker, and possibly lose the small stake I was carrying home, I contented myself in the evenings by reading a book and reflecting on my experiences as skipper of the now defunct 107th Battalion. Anyway, I enjoyed my stay with Steve Gulledge and his friends.

## USS *Griggs* (En Route to San Diego)

On November 2, 1945, I boarded the USS *Griggs* for transportation to San Francisco. I thanked Captain Ware and my friend Lt. Cmdr. Steve Gulledge for making my two-week stay on Saipan a pleasant experience. As I boarded this navy transport and prepared to depart Saipan and the Marianas, I could not help but reflect that if the war had not ended, I would be going ashore at the tip end of Kyushu, Japan, with the 107th right about this [planned] date as part of Operation Olympic. Should President Truman have given the green light for dropping the atom bomb[s] in Japan? I just did not know. But I do know that I was going home instead of leading my battalion into the Japanese homeland as a part of a planned invasion. Reality supersedes philosophy.[14]

We left Saipan on November 2, 1945, loaded to the gills with military personnel heading home. We were crowded on the ship, the food was not gourmet, and the sea was rough—but all this did not matter. We were going home. I had orders for separation at Camp Wallace, between Houston and Galveston, which would be my next—and final—duty station before returning to civilian life. On my arrival in San Francisco, Jeannette and I could drive her little Chevrolet across the country for her to meet my parents in Rosenberg—and then to Camp Wallace to be released from active duty. During this period, I would still be on active duty—and on the payroll. Then I would have 90 days terminal leave. I would, of course, make the trip in uniform.

On the ship I shared quarters with the former skipper of the 110th Seabees. Most of his junior officers, including warrant officers, were on board. I was the only member of the old 107th Seabees aboard. The junior officers were in steerage, with bunks four deep.

14. Like most Pacific veterans and Americans in 1945 and after, my grandfather always said that the atomic bombs saved his life, because they ended the war sooner rather than later, which would have resulted in many more American (and Japanese) dead.

It was hot down there, and they had trouble getting enough sleep, so during the day they could come up in shifts to use our bunks to catch up on their sleep. I did not complain; however, I would have enjoyed an afternoon siesta, but my bunk was in use. I felt sorry for the junior officers in their crowded quarters.

Our transport was passing north of Midway Island when we received some news that was disturbing to me. We were officially informed that we would not be going into San Francisco, as originally planned, but rather to San Diego. This would be our disembarkation port. This presented me with a problem. I would need to arrange transportation from San Diego to San Francisco in order to travel to Texas with my wife. Somehow, I felt this could be worked out on our arrival at San Diego. During the following days at sea, I had time to reflect on how this change of plans would further delay my reunion with Jeannette. No one bothered to explain the change of ports for our disembarkation.

## San Diego

On November 15, 1945, the USS *Griggs* sailed into San Diego harbor. Although I had been in the Merchant Marine earlier, this was my first visit to this harbor. It is truly a beautiful place. We docked and were immediately transferred by bus with our gear to an Intake Station. I went to see the lieutenant-commander in charge of the station to inquire about transportation to San Francisco to meet my wife and carry out my basic plan to go to Camp Wallace, my next duty station. He greeted me with open arms and told me he had been waiting for me to arrive. He planned to place me in charge of a train, loaded with sailors, who were here and headed for Camp Wallace for separation. I could not think of a more undesirable assignment. Imagine being responsible for a bunch of wild sailors on a train going back to Texas. Also, how about my wife waiting in San Francisco for my arrival? I put up a brave front, hardened by duty in the Aleutians and the Pacific, and bluntly told the lieutenant commander that I had changed my mind about Camp Wallace and decided to be separated in Los Angeles. I expected him to say he could not change my basic orders and I would have to accept command of the troop train to Texas. To my surprise—and delight—he turned to his yeoman and said "Modify Commander Ritter's Orders for Separation in Los Angeles."

## Oceanside, California

The lieutenant-commander in command of the Intake Station at
Oceanside really gave me a pleasant surprise when he gave me
a modified set of orders to change my separation center to Los
Angeles, rather than Camp Wallace, Texas. Now I did not have to
worry about the sailors on the troop train headed for Texas. Also,
I would be able to join Jeannette in San Francisco shortly and drive
to Rosenberg to see my folks. The C.O. of the Intake Station told
me to get a good night's sleep and arranged for me to catch an early
train the next day for Los Angeles. I called Jeannette by phone—no
easy task at this stage—to tell her where I was and the change of
plans. She was disappointed that I had not landed in San Francisco,
but was happy I would be there in a few days—at which time we
would plan our trip to Rosenberg.

## Los Angeles

I caught an early train from Oceanside to Los Angeles. On
November 16, 1945, I reported to the separation center there.
On the next day, November 17, I was detached and separated with
90 days terminal leave, or until February 12, 1946, when I would
be completely released from the navy (after almost four years).
Then they paid me off—$1,000 in $100 bills. I did not care to carry
this much cash on me around Los Angeles, so I went to the Bank of
America and got some travelers cheques. The center also gave me
a $100 travel allowance; however, they could not find me any way
to travel to San Francisco. At this particular time, plane and train
reservations were at a premium due to the immense travel load of
returning servicemen. I talked to Jeannette by phone. She said she
would use her influence to get me on a train for San Francisco.

Two days passed and I was still stuck in Los Angeles. Then
Jeannette called to say she thought she had it arranged for me
to catch the Southern Pacific "Daylight" for San Francisco the
following day. Then, just on a hunch, I dropped into the United
Airlines Office, and to my great surprise, they said they had space
for me on a flight to San Francisco. I immediately called Jeannette
to advise her of my good fortune and my expected arrival by air in
San Francisco.

# Epilogue: November 18, 1945

## *San Francisco*

On November 18, 1945, I stepped off a United Airlines plane at Mills Field [San Francisco International Airport]. I could see Jeannette waiting for me behind a chain link fence as I left the plane. It had been such a long time[1] since she told me goodbye as I boarded a seaplane [the Clipper] at Treasure Island on February 24, 1944—almost two years. It was so good to see her again and to renew our married life—hopefully never to be separated again.

---

1. Which was also the title of the sentimental 1945 song "It's Been a Long, Long Time" about veterans returning to their loved ones after the war.

# Conclusion (1945–1994)

O n November 30, 1945, Rex was finally promoted to full Commander, CEC, USNR, by Commander Neil Kingsley. Then he and my grandmother went on their second honeymoon to Texas, where my grandfather introduced her to his family. He wrote that his family made my grandmother "feel like a full-fledged member of the Ritter Clan." After that they went to New Orleans and then back to Texas to celebrate Christmas 1945 with his family, where my grandmother knew that she had been accepted as a full member of the Ritter family, just as my grandfather had been accepted by her parents in 1943. They also celebrated my great-grandparents' 46th wedding anniversary on New Year's Eve, 1945.

After my grandparents returned to San Francisco in early 1946, he began looking for a job before his postwar terminal leave was up. In February 1946, he began working as an engineer for the San Francisco Housing Authority, which was building new homes for veterans and their families due to the postwar housing shortage. He felt that staying and working in San Francisco would be the wisest thing to do, rather than commuting to work outside the city.[1]

1. Ed Nichols, who was an Assistant Superintendent in the San Francisco Unified School District and a friend of my grandmother from school, told my grandfather in

That was when he knew that he would not be going back to work for the Texas State Highway Department in Wichita Falls. His terminal leave expired on February 12, 1946.

Thus ended his activities during the war years, from the Aleutians to the Central Pacific, since 1942. Although this concluded his active duty status as a naval reserve officer, he remained a commissioned officer as a commander in the naval reserves, but he did not plan to take part in any of the naval reserve programs, so he could concentrate on his new civilian job.

Over a year later, in June 1947, Roger T. Ritter (my father), the only son of Rex and Jeannette, was born in San Francisco. My grandfather stayed in the naval reserves and eventually rose to the rank of captain. He was recalled to active duty during the Korean War, but due to his age and the fact that he had a family, he was assigned to the Federal Building in San Francisco. Later he worked as a civilian employee for the Navy Department, becoming Director of Maintenance for the 12th Naval District, all the while remaining in the reserves. Contrary to his earlier plans, he participated in weekend reserve drills on Treasure Island Naval Station in San Francisco Bay, and every summer he did a two-week training duty at naval bases in California, Nevada, and Washington State. My father recalls that his summer vacations always coincided with those training duties, which was not bad at all, since they generally went to the seaside, to places such as Coronado in Southern California and Whidbey Island in the San Juan Islands, a beautiful place between Washington State and British Columbia.

My grandfather retired from the naval reserves on New Year's Day, 1963, and from his federal civilian employment in 1965.[2] Jeannette died in 1992 and Rex died in 1994. They were buried together at Cypress Lawn Memorial Cemetery in Colma, California.

He was buried in his uniform.

---

early 1946 that the Italians owned the city (the Bank of America, formerly the Bank of Italy, was the largest bank), and the Irish ran it (they had staffed the police force and the civil service since the late 19th century). That was before the postwar demographic changes in the city and the Bay Area after the 1950s and the 1960s.

2. He told my father that he could have retired as a "tombstone admiral," *i.e.*, as a rear-admiral, provided that he give up his pension and other retiree benefits. Preferring those benefits to a title, however grand, and true to the old Texas adage that "his mama didn't raise no stupid children," he retired as a captain and kept the benefits.

# Appendices

## U.S. Navy Commissioned Officer Ranks

Ensign (ENS)
Lieutenant (Junior Grade) (LTJG)
Lieutenant (LT)
Lieutenant Commander (LCDR)
Commander (CDR)
Captain (CAPT)
Rear Admiral (lower half) (RDML)
Rear Admiral (upper half) (RADM)
Vice Admiral (VADM)
Admiral (ADM)
Fleet Admiral (FADM)*

* The rank of Fleet Admiral has been reserved for wartime use only. The last Fleet Admirals were created during World War II. They were as follows: Chester W. Nimitz, William D. Leahy, Ernest J. King, and William F. Halsey. (http://www.navy.mil/navydata/ranks/officers/o-rank.html)

## Naval and Military Terms

BOQ (Bachelor Officers' Quarters)
CEC (Civil Engineer Corps)
CINCPAC (Commander-in-Chief-Pacific Fleet)
O.D. (Officer-of-the-Day)
OINC (Officer in Charge)

## The Song of the Seabees

We're the Seabees of the Navy
We can build and we can fight
We'll pave a way to victory
And guard it day and night
And we promise that we'll remember the "Seventh of December"
We're the Seabees of the Navy
The bees of the Seven Seas.

166

—Song of the Seabees (1942)—*Naval Construction Battalions Civil Engineer Corps Facilities Engineering Command Anniversary Ball* (Program, 1967)

## WWII Honor Roll (National WWII Memorial)

James Rex Ritter

BRANCH OF SERVICE
U.S. Naval Reserve

HOMETOWN
Wichita Falls, TX

HONORED BY
Jonathan Ritter, Grandson

ACTIVITY DURING WWII

NAVY SEABEE.

The WWII Registry (https://www.wwiimemorial.com/Registry/Search.aspx)

Anyone may log onto the registry and honor the name of a World War II veteran or someone who contributed to the war effort on the home front. I have also added the names of my maternal grandfather, Anthony Kutch, a skilled airplane craftsman who built airplanes on the home front in Long Island, New York, and my great-uncle, Emile Adrian Rouyet, a USAAF sergeant and airplane mechanic in Brazil, to the WWII Registry.

# References
# and Further Reading

Ritter Family World War II collection (1942–1945): Documents, maps (*Pacific Ocean and the Bay of Bengal*) (National Geographic, 1943), letters, 107th Seabee scrapbook (1943–1944), 107th *Pipeline* newsletter (1944–1945), photos, medals.

## *Books and Other Secondary Sources*

"107th Naval Construction Battalion *Historical Information.*" *Naval History & Heritage Command.*

Ambrose, Hugh. *The Pacific*. NAL Caliber and HBO, 2009, 2011.

Baime, A.J. *The Accidental President: Harry S. Truman and the First Four Months That Changed the World*. Boston: Houghton Mifflin Harcourt, 2017.

Ballard, Robert D. *Graveyards of the Pacific: From Pearl Harbor to Bikini Atoll*. Washington, D.C.: National Geographic, Odyssey Enterprises, 2001.

Bluhm Jr., Col. Raymond K, ed, USA (Ret.) *World War II: A Chronology of War*. New York: Beaux Arts Editions and Universe Publishing, 2017.

Brown, DeSoto. *Hawaii Goes to War: Life in Hawaii From Pearl Harbor to Peace*. Honolulu, HI: Editions Limited, 1989.

Castillo, Edmund L, USN. *The Seabees of World War II*. New York: Random House and Landmark Books, 1963.

Cohen, Stan. *The Pink Palace: Royal Hawaiian, Waikiki*. Missoula, MT: Pictorial Histories Publishing Company, Inc., 1986.

Compston, Christine, and Rachel Filene Sideman, eds. Foreword by Michael Beschloss. *Our Documents: 100 Milestone Documents from the National Archives*. New York: Oxford University Press, Inc., 2003.

Cowley, Robert, ed. *No End Save Victory: Perspectives on World War II*. New York: Berkeley Books, 2001.

Craven, Wesley Frank, and James Lea Cate. *The Army Air Forces in World War II* (5 vols.). Washington, D.C.: University of Chicago Press and the University of Toronto Press, Office of Air Force History, U.S. Government Printing Office, 1948–1953, 1983.

DeConde, Alexander. *A History of American Foreign Policy*. New York: Charles Scribner's Sons, 1963.

Editors of American Heritage. *The American Heritage Pictorial Atlas of United States History*. New York: The American Heritage Publishing Co., Inc., 1966.

*The End of World War II: Official Surrender Document Signed in Tokyo Bay, Japan, September 2, 1945. Signed on Board the Battleship USS* Missouri *by Representatives of the Allied Forces and the Japanese Empire*. Fredericksburg, TX: The Awani Press, 1981.

Farrell, Don A. *Tinian*. Tinian, MP: Micronesian Publications, CNMI, 1992.

_____. *Tinian and the Bomb: Project Alberta and Operation Centerboard*. Tinian, MP: University of Guam Press and Micronesian Publications, 2018.

Frank, Richard B. *Downfall: The End of the Imperial Japanese Empire*. New York: Penguin Books, 1999, 2001.

*Freedom from Fear: FDR Commander in Chief*. Hyde Park, NY: Franklin D. Roosevelt Library and Museum, Sept. 2, 2005–Nov. 5, 2006.

Garvy, John, and the California Center for Military History. *Images of America— San Francisco in World War II*. Charleston, SC: Arcadia Publishing, 2007.

Goldstein, Donald M., Katherine V. Dillon and J. Michael Wenger. *Rain of Ruin: A Photographic History of Hiroshima and Nagasaki* (America at War Series). Washington: Brassey's, 1995.

Hansen, Gladys. *San Francisco Almanac: Everything You Want to Know about the City*. San Rafael, CA: Presidio Press, 1980.

Hornfischer, James D. *America at Total War in the Pacific, 1944–1945*. New York: Bantam Books, 2016.

Huie, William Bradford, CEC, USNR. *Can Do! The Story of the Seabees*. New York: E.P Dutton & Company, Inc., 1944, 1945.

———. *From Omaha to Okinawa: The Story of the Seabees*. New York: E.P Dutton & Company, Inc., 1945.

Krowe, Michelle A. *The World War II Memorial: Honoring the Price of Freedom*. Virginia Beach, VA: Eastern National and The Donning Company Publishers, 2007.

Lockwood, Charles A. *Tragedy at Honda*. 1960; repr. Annapolis, MD: Naval Institute Press, 2012.

*The Log of the 107th Seabees, 1943–1945: A Story of a Seabee Battalion Conceived in War … Dedicated to Peace*. Baton Rouge, LA: 107th Naval Construction Battalion and Navy Pictorial Publishers, 1946. Digitized version online.

*Making Peace: The Legacy of Hiroshima and Nagasaki: A Teacher's Guide Grades 4–12*. Hiroshima and Nagasaki 50th Anniversary Commemoration Committee and National Japanese Historical Society, July 1995.

Marston, Daniel, ed. *The Pacific War Companion: From Pearl Harbor to Hiroshima*. Oxford, UK: Osprey Press, 2005.

Martin, Dan. *Pearl Harbor Inside Guide* (Foldout). Honolulu, HI: Bess Press, Inc., 2005, 2008.

———. *Pearl Harbor: History. Highlights. Facts* (Foldout). Bess Press, Inc., 2016.

Mawdsley, Evan. *December 1941: Twelve Days That Began a World War*. New Haven: Yale University Press, 2011.

McDevitt, Lt. Comdr. E.A., USNR, ed. *The Naval History of Treasure Island*. San Francisco: U.S. Naval Training and Distribution Center, 1946.

McCullough, David. *Truman*. New York: Simon & Schuster, 1992.

Moynahan, Brian. *The French Century*. Paris: Flammarion, 2007.

Pedisich, Paul E. *Congress Buys a Navy*. Annapolis, Maryland: Naval Institute Press, 2016.

Polmar, Norman. *The Enola Gay: The B-29 That Dropped the Atomic Bomb on Hiroshima*. Washington, D.C.: Brassey's Inc., and the Smithsonian National Air and Space Museum, 2004.

Potter. E.B. *Nimitz*. Annapolis, MD: Naval Institute Press, 1976.

"Remembering V-J Day, August 15, 1945." www.nationalww2museum.org

Reynolds, David. *Rich Relations: The American Occupation of Britain 1942–1945*. HarperCollins and Phoenix Press, 1995.

Rigge, Simon, and the Editors of Time-Life Books. *War in the Outposts*. Alexandria, VA: Time-Life Books, World War II Series, 1980.

Rogers, J. David. "U.S. Navy Seabees During World War II." https://web.mst.
    edu/~rogersda/umrcourses/ge342/SeaBees-Revised.pdf
Ronck, Ronn. *Battleship Missouri: The Battleship Missouri in Pearl Harbor,
    Hawai'i*. Honolulu, HI: Mutual Publishing, 1999.
Schnoebelen, Anne. *Treasures: Splendid Survivors of the Golden Gate Interna-
    tional Exposition* (Booklet). Berkeley, CA: GGIE Research Associates and the
    Treasure Island Museum Association, 1991, 2009.
"Seabee History: Formation of the Seabees in World War II." http://www.history.
    navy.mil
*Smithsonian World War II: The Definitive Visual History from Blitzkrieg to the
    Atom Bomb*. New York: DK Publishing, 2009, 2015.
Starr, Kevin. *Embattled Dreams: California in War and Peace, 1940–1950*
    (Americans and the California Dream series). New York: Oxford University
    Press, 2002.
Steinberg, Rafael, and the Editors of Time-Life Books. *Island Fighting*. Alexandria,
    VA: Time-Life Books (World War II series), 1978.
Tibbets, Paul W. *Return of the Enola Gay*. Columbus, OH: A Paul Tibbets Book
    and Mid Coast Marketing, 1998.
Tillman, Barrett. *Whirlwind: The Air War Against Japan 1942–1945*. New York:
    Simon & Schuster, 2010.
Toll, Ian. *The Conquering Tide: War in the Pacific Islands, 1942–1944*. New York:
    W.W. Norton & Company, 2015.
Trudell, Clyde. *Colonial Yorktown: Being a Brief Historie of the Place; Together
    with Something of Its Houses and Publick Buildings*. Richmond, VA: The Dietz
    Press, Publishers, 1938.
*The Westin St. Francis: Celebrating a Century of History on Union Square*
    (Booklet). San Francisco, CA: The Westin St. Francis, 2006.
Wheeler, Keith. *The Pacific Is My Beat*. New York: E.P. Dutton and Company,
    Inc., 1943.
_____. And the Editors of Time-Life Books. *The Fall of Japan*. Alexandria, VA:
    Time-Life Books (World War II series), 1983.
Whitworth, Kieran. *The Ultimate World War II Quiz Book: 1,000 Questions
    and Answers to Test Your Knowledge*. Michael O'Hara and Imperial War
    Museums, 2017.
*World War II Day by Day*. London: Dorling Kindersley Limited, 2001; originally
    published as *Chronicle of the Second World War* in 1990.
Zich, Arthur, and the Editors of Time-Life Books. *The Rising Sun*. World War II
    Series. Alexandria, VA: Time-Life Books, 1977.

## *Articles and Periodicals*

*America in WWII Special 65th Anniversary* (August 2010).
*Bureau of Naval Personnel Information Bulletin* (December 1943, May 1945).
Camp, Richard (Colonel, USMC, Ret.) "Taking Tinian." *WWII Quarterly* 10, no. 2
    (Winter 2019): 64–77.
Correll, John T. "The Smithsonian and the *Enola Gay*." http://www.airforcemag.
    com (April 2004): 2–27.
_____. "The *Enola Gay* and the Smithsonian Chronology of the Controversy
    1993–1995."

Correll, John T. *"Enola Gay* Archive: AFA's *Enola Gay* Archive Collection: The Smithsonian and the *Enola Gay*: Frequently Asked Questions."

"Don't Come to San Francisco Now" (1943). *Western Neighborhood Project Newsletter* (Fall 2005): 7.

"Extra: Now It's Official: Japan Surrenders.," "M'Arthur Named Jap Boss," "Japanese Accept Victors' Terms." *San Jose News*, August 14, 1945.

Frank, Richard B. "Why Truman Dropped the Bomb." *The Weekly Standard* 20, no. 44 (August 8, 2005): 20–24.

Hallon, Richard P. "Operation Starvation." *World War II* 23, no. 1 (April/May 2008): 48–55.

*Honoring the Past, Inspiring the Future: 75th Anniversary of the Attack on Pearl Harbor*. Autodesk, Inc., 2016.

Matus, Victorino. *"The Pacific." On Patrol: The Magazine of the USO* 1, no. 4 (Winter 2009–2010): 22–28.

Morelock, Jeffrey D. "American Warlords: MacArthur, Eisenhower and Nimitz." *Armchair General* 9, no. 3 (July 2012): 21–27.

"Peace: Shooting Ends in Pacific," "Truman Names MacArthur To Head Jap Occupation," "U.S. Cruiser Sunk [USS *Indianapolis*]." *Pittsburgh Sun-Telegraph*, August 15, 1945.

"Pieces of History: Victory! Americans Everywhere Celebrated the End of World War II in 1945." https://prologue.blogs.archives.gov, September 2, 2015: 1–4.

"Second World War: USA: The United States in the Second World War." Imperial War Museum (IWM). http://www.theirpast-yourfuture.org.uk

"Special 70th Anniversary Edition: 1945–2015: WWIII. America Comes Home." *USA Today Special Edition*, 2015.

*Time V-J Day: 60th Anniversary Tribute: America's World War II Triumph in the Pacific* (Time Inc. Specials). Time Inc. Home Entertainment, 2005.

_____.*Time 1945–2010 65th Anniversary Tribute: Visions of Victory: America's Triumph in World War II*. Time Inc. Home Entertainment, 2010.

_____.*Time: 1945: The Year That Changed the World*. Time Inc. Books, 2015.

_____. *Time-Life World War II: Victory in the Pacific: The End of to a Ferocious Conflict*. Time Inc. Books, 2016.

"War! Oahu Bombed by Japanese Planes." *Honolulu Star-Advertiser*, December 7, 1941.

"Voices of World War II." *Newsweek*, March 8, 1999.

## *Articles in the* San Francisco Chronicle

Flinn, John. "Travel: Hiroshima at Peace." July 31, 2005.

"List of Events for Service People." July 1, August 26, 1945.

Nolte, Carl. "San Francisco: Pearl Harbor Was a Close Thing for the City in 1941: There Was Fear and Panic— Reports of Flares, a Japanese Sub Offshore, Planes Nearing." December 7, 2006.

_____. "How Pearl Harbor Ended up Reshaping the Bay Area." December 7, 2011.

_____. "The Dark Side of V-J Day: The Story of the City's Deadliest Riot Had Been Largely Forgotten." August 15, 2005.

Orderly V-J Night: Bars Close, Crowds Are Quiet as S.F. Greets Surrender Signing." September 2, 1945.

## *Articles in* The Wall Street Journal

Borneman, Walter R. "Books: Supreme Sacrifice." September 1–2, 2018.
Rosenberg, Elliot. "Opinion: *Navy Day in New York, 1945*." October 26, 2015.

## *Articles in* U.S. News & World Report

Fang, Bay. "Letter from Hiroshima, Japan: Rethinking the Bomb." December 4, 2006: 34.
Hayden, Thomas. "Museums: Udvar-Hazy Keeps Me Hanging On." December 29, 2003/January 5, 2004: D-4.
Parshall, Gerald. "Special Report: 50 Years Later: Hiroshima: The Shock Wave." Vol. 119, No. 5, July 31, 1995: 44–59.

## *Articles in* American Heritage

Dobell, Byron. "V-J, 1945." Vol. 36, no. 5 (August/September 1985): 7.
Ferrell, Robert F., ed. "Truman at Potsdam." Vol. 31, No. 4 (June/July 1980): 36–47.
Maddox, Robert James. "The Biggest Decision: Why We Had to Drop the Bomb.," James A Field, Jr. "Tokyo, 1945." Vol. 46, issue 3 (May/June 1995): 1–11.
_____. "History Now: Hiroshima Re-considered: A New Book Makes a Persuasive Case for Our Use of Atomic Bombs." (August/September 2004): 14.
Rotter, Andrew J. "Atomic Aftermath." August 25, 2008: 1–3.
Squires, Vernon C. "Landing at Tokyo Bay." Vol. 36, No. 5 (August/September 1985): 24–33.

## *Articles in* National Geographic

Gup, Ted. "Hiroshima." Vol. 188, No. 2 (August 1995): 78–101.
Poole, Robert M. "Japan's Imperial Palace: Beyond the Moat." Vol. 199, No. 1 (January 2001): 94–123.

## *Websites*

National WWII Memorial, Washington, D.C. https://www.wwiimemorial.com/
National Museum of the Pacific War. http://www.pacificwarmuseum.org/
World War II Valor in the Pacific. https://www.nps.gov/valr/index.htm
"Office of the Historian: Milestones: 1937–1945: Diplomacy at the Road to Another War." https://history.state.gov
_____. "Japan, China, the United States and the Road to Pearl Harbor, 1937–41."
"Timeline: The War in the Pacific, 1944–1945 (*Victory in the Pacific*)." http://www.pbs.org/wgbh/americanexperience
https://ussmissouri.org/learn-the-history/surrender
Seabee Museum and Memorial Park, Rhode Island.
https://www.seabeesmuseum.com/seabee-history
https://www.seabeesmuseum.com/visit/quonset-huts
http://www.members.tripod.com/airfields_freeman/HI/Airfields_W_Pacific.htm#northfield
"Harry S. Truman: The Presidential Years: The First Four Months, Decision to Drop the Bomb, Postwar America." https://www.trumanlibrary.org/hst/
_____. https://www.trumanlibrary.org/publicpapers/index.php?pid=107

"Chronology of San Francisco War Events: 1940–41: Treasure Island to Pearl
    Harbor, 1942: Japanese Internment to Guadalcanal, 1943: Aleutians Campaign
    to V-Home Campaign, 1945: Iwo Jima to Japan's Capitulation." http://www.
    sfmuseum.org/1906/ww2.html
"Treasure Island Museum Association: Pan Am Clippers, U.S. Navy, Treasure
    Island Museum." http://tima.mobi/statues/lobbygallery
http://usnhistory.navylive.dodlive.mil/2017/03/03/10-things-you-need-to-know-
    about-your-seabees/
https://www.history.navy.mil/research/library/online-reading-room/title-list-
    alphabetically/s/seabee-history0/world-war-ii.html
U.S. Navy Seabee Museum https://www.history.navy.mil/content/dam/museums/
    Seabee/UnitListPages/NCB/107%20NCB.pdf
https://www.stripes.com/news/2nd-pearl-harbor-kept-top-secret-until-1962-
    commemorated-1.410773

## *Documentaries, Movies and Newsreels*

*Admiral Chester Nimitz: Thunder of the Pacific* (A&E *Biography*, 1996). Part of
    the *Pearl Harbor* (also titled *Tora Tora Tora: The True Story of Pearl Harbor*)
    (2000) History Channel DVD set.
"Japan: 1941–1945," "Pacific: February 1942–July 1945," "The Bomb: February–
    September 1945." *The World at War* (Thames Television, 1974).
*The Last Bomb* (1945).
*Last Flight of Bomber 31* (*Nova*, 2003).
*MacArthur* (*American Experience*, 1999).
*MacArthur* (1977). Biopic about General MacArthur (Gregory Peck) and his life
    between 1942–1952 and 1962.
"Navy Day 1945 in New York City" (October 1945).
*San Francisco in the Forties* (also titled *San Francisco in the 1940s*) (KRON,
    1986).
*Target Tokyo* (1945).
*Truman* (*American Experience*, 1997)
"Truman reads the letter from the Japanese government. Nation celebrates.
    Gas rationing ends." (*Universal Newsreel*, August 1945).
*Victory in the Pacific* (*American Experience*, 2005).

# Index